A TRUE STORY

Beloved Outcast

The Quest for True Belonging

CHERIE DENNA

What people are saying about **Beloved Outcast**

Beloved Outcast is a captivating and intimate story which illuminates God's overwhelming love and redemption. Cherie Denna enthralls us with her extraordinary account of navigating from a childhood enmeshed in a mob family and outlaw biker clubs to answering God's call to spread the Gospel. Amidst the backdrop of mystery, intrigue, and betrayal, this true story grants us profound insight into God's relentless rescue mission. *Beloved Outcast* is a must-read for those trapped in seemingly inescapable circumstances who desire a victorious life of freedom. This is a book you won't be able to put down!

—Charlene D. Quint, Esq.
Founder at AbuseCare.org

A mesmerizing tale of truth and conviction. There is nothing more powerful than true humility when it is God inspired. Cherie Denna gives us a glimpse into a prodigal story of redemption. God always has a better plan for our lives if we allow Him to lead and we truly follow. *Beloved Outcast* is a powerful story of His grace and glory.

—Johnny Lujan
Pastor, Thunder Road Biker Church

In *Beloved Outcast*, author Cherie Denna uses her own life to illustrate how intimately God loves each of us. Through looking back at her early life in humble transparency, the author is able to let us see God's fingerprints and covering in the worst of circumstances. By sharing her story, she enables us all to see God at work in our own lives.

—Edie Melson
Author and Director
of Blue Ridge Mountains Christian Writers Conference

Beloved Outcast is a powerful and inspiring memoir that chronicles the author's journey from a life of violence and uncertainty to her discovery of faith in God. Cherie's brutal honesty and raw vulnerability make this book a captivating read that will resonate with those seeking hope and redemption. Her story is a testament to the power of faith and the triumph of the human spirit.

—Chuck Wysong
Executive Director
of Mission Springs Camps and Conference Center

Through adept storytelling and vulnerability, Cherie Denna takes us on a journey of self-discovery, revealing the profound impact our own childhood experiences have on our identity. *Beloved Outcast* leads us along the author's quest to escape from that, unveiling how we can seek solace and undergo transformation through the healing power of God. This book will empower readers to redefine their own stories, overcome self-destructive patterns, find freedom from guilt, and endure with unrelenting faith. Even after you've finished reading and put this book down, this story will remain in your heart forever.

—Phylis Mantelli
Host, The Unmothered Podcast

In *Beloved Outcast*, Cherie Denna skillfully and honestly takes the reader through the raw and raunchy times that repeatedly drew her back into a life she knew so well, yet earnestly wanted to escape. Her storytelling will mesmerize readers, rendering them incapable of abandoning the book as they fervently support Cherie in triumphing over the ancestral hurdles and tribulations. This book is for all who have ever felt outcast and unworthy and for anyone who wants to break free of the strongholds of the past. It's also a story of God's second chances. This remarkable tale reminds us that God never gives up seeking and saving the lost.

—Janet Thompson
www.womantowomanmentoring.com

The captivating narrative of *Beloved Outcast* invites readers to immerse themselves in the enthralling journey of Cherie's life. Every word of her story pulls you in, keeping you fully absorbed until the very end. This compelling memoir is a poignant must-read for individuals seeking a sense of connection and purpose. Through Cherie's story, readers are transported beyond the boundaries of past traumas, as they discover the transformative power of a relationship with Jesus. Like a beacon in the darkness, this book illuminates the path to profound connection and true belonging, inspiring all who read it.

—B.J. Garrett
Author, *Unwanted No More:*
From Exploited to Embraced by God

Even more compelling than *The Cross and the Switchblade*—*Beloved Outcast* is not only a must-read, but this book also needs to make it to the big screen.

— Amber Weigand-Buckley
Founding Editor of multi-award-winning
Leading Hearts Magazine

Beloved Outcast

The Quest for True Belonging

CHERIE DENNA

Abundance Books

Editor: Larry J. Leech II
Cover Design by Amber Wiegand-Buckley, Barefaced Media
Interior design by WendyEL Creative

Published in the United States of America.
Abundance Books LLC
Kalamazoo, MI

*It takes great courage to rightly judge the
evil that has wounded us…
Yet not judge the wounded soul through
whom the evil comes.*

Shadia Hrichi
Author of
Hagar: Rediscovering the God Who Sees Me

*In memory of my sister, Jami Ann
LaLanne-Clark, who learned to cry joyful tears.
The last weeks of her life outshined the rest.
October 28, 1965–November 9, 1992*

*The righteous cry out, and the LORD hears
them; he delivers them from all their troubles.
Psalm 34:17*

Note from the Author

I wrote this memoir from memory. Because of my struggle with both repressed and suppressed memories, I relied on family and friends to provide some details that I added to the story.

Out of respect and privacy for several individuals and organizations, I changed numerous names and re-created some scenes with my best recollection.

Regarding dialogue, not everything is verbatim unless the words made such an impact that I could reproduce the conversation word for word. This also applies to the people whom I describe to the best of my ability, considering memory issues, my age at the time many of these events occurred, and my impressions at that moment. Family and friends may not recollect events as I have.

This is my story and nobody else's.

Chapter 1

The deep gold-and-black shag carpet failed to mask the bone-rattling vibrations while the bikers rode their motorcycles up the steep driveway into our yard. Their headlights pierced through every front window. My stomach knotted up.

Mama hurried from the kitchen to her room at the end of the hallway. She put on her favorite pair of black leather pants. Her eyes, a tranquil light blue, and captivating outlined in black. Easily mistaken for Priscilla Presley's twin, Mama's hair may have stood higher. She dashed back to the kitchen, hopping from one foot to the other into her high heeled black leather boots, transforming her petite five-foot-four frame into a statuesque Sicilian beauty.

I hugged her leg with one hand, my ear pressed tight against her pant leg while she transferred the pasta pot of boiling noodles to the sink. The vibration from the floor jumped right into my vocal cords. "Mama, it's so loud. Make them leave, Mama."

Her voice raised with concern while pouring the scalding water. "Watch out, sweetie. I'm in a hurry, and I don't want to burn you." She glanced over her shoulder. "And don't be silly. Go get your sister."

I hurried from the kitchen around the end of the dark hallway into our bedroom. Jami sat Indian style on the giant pillow Mama sewed to match our blankets. The fluorescent colors glowed beneath the black light mounted on the bedroom wall, which Mama painted in my favorite shade of purple. My sister's head of blonde Shirley Temple curls hid her face. She focused on the castle made of wood blocks stacked on the lavender shag carpet.

I waved my hand sharply in circles. "Time to wash up for dinner." I glanced out the bedroom door toward the living room. The bikers were still outside. I hope they stay out there.

We scurried across the hallway into the bathroom. I closed and locked the door in case someone tried to come in. At three years old, Jami barely reached the faucet. We dried our wet hands on our shorts, and took our seats at the small, oval wood-grain laminate kitchen table. Mama glanced out the kitchen window and nodded to someone while she dished the macaroni with gravy into our bowls. I took Jami's hand.

Mama handed us our dinner. "Okay, you girls are gonna eat in your room tonight. Remember, only come out if you need to go potty. Understand?"

Pouting, we both agreed. When my father lived with us, we ate at the table. At least we ate at the kid's table with our cousins at our great-grandmother's Sunday dinners.

I nearly dropped my bowl while I hurried to our bedroom. "C'mon, Jami. You heard Mama."

Mama trailed behind us. At the doorway, she kissed us on the tops of our heads. I always loved when she did that. She motioned us into the room and shut the door. Her voice faint, she said, "You girls be good."

After Jami and I finished dinner, we lay back on the bottom bunk, Jami's head at one end and mine at the other. Led Zeppelin's "Dazed and Confused" blared from the living room. Loud voices combined with men's laughter invaded our attempt to fall asleep.

Jami gasped and grabbed my leg when a loud bang shook the walls. I patted her hand. "Close your eyes. We aren't taking a bath tonight." She turned onto her side, faced the wall, and twirled her curls in her fingers.

The party carried on late into the night. Nervous another fight would erupt, I hugged my pillow tight. An occasional thud against the bedroom door told me to ignore the urge to go potty.

I woke the next morning grateful I'd slept through the night without nightmares. I pressed my ear against the bedroom door. Nothing. I opened the door slowly. Our house smelled like smoke, but it wasn't cigarette smoke. I started toward the bathroom directly across the hall. A man yelled bad words from the living room. My curiosity got the best of me. I held my breath and tiptoed closer to the end of the hall to get a better view. I kneeled behind the black wrought-iron wall divider and gripped the cold metal to steady myself. The black walls and black and gold carpet darkened the room.

A tall man with long black hair pulled tight into a ponytail stood with his back to me. He wore Levi's and a black leather vest with patches on it over a black T-shirt. He plunged his black steel-toed boot into the back of the man lying on the couch. He yelled at him to get up. I squealed with fright, then covered my mouth. The man on the couch pulled his knees to his chest and rocked back and forth, covering his ribs with his arms. I couldn't see his face. Another man, not so tall but much huskier, barged in the front door with the garden hose and doused water over the poor man's face.

Mama spotted me crouched down in the hallway when she bolted from the kitchen. The jerking gesture of her hand warned me to stay put. When she yelled at the man with the hose, the two bikers dragged the man off the couch, down the concrete porch steps, and threw him into the dirt. The water from the hose continued to flood his eyes, nose, and mouth.

Mama stood in the middle of the living room, seething with anger while she assessed the mess they'd made. The chaos outside quickly shifted her attention. I'm not sure what she thought she could do to stop the brutality, but she bolted outside and slammed the front door. I'd imagine she worried about the cops showing up.

I snuck to the living room window. The two men drug the man across the rocky dirt yard, down the driveway, and lifted him onto our neighbor's concrete retaining wall. He fell from the ledge on his face. Blood spattered all over the sidewalk. I guessed I wouldn't sit up there and talk to my neighbor, Johnny, after that. Mama never liked it when I did. She thought I might fall and hurt myself.

Mama yelled, "Get him out of here, now."

I hoped one of the neighbors would call the police but help never came. Somehow, the bloodied man managed to lift himself up from the pavement. The two bikers who had pulled him outside put him into a truck and drove off. I didn't understand how my mother could look at the bikers as trusted protectors, as family. I did not see them that way.

Their presence in our house created an atmosphere of fear, vulnerability, and insecurity. And the outlaw biker culture would become an all-encompassing presence in my life for the next twelve years.

Chapter 2

Jami and I made the most of the day, alternating between reading and playing games in the backyard. I preferred to escape to my room with my dozens of books. Mama sometimes hid them to encourage me to play outside.

After several hours, the throaty echo of motorcycle exhaust drew me back to reality. I covered my ears tight with both hands when the bikes charged into our garage. With my eyes squeezed shut, my heart pounded hard in my chest. I ran to the kitchen. Not again. Jami trailed behind.

The motorcycles were always loud, but this sounded like an army arriving in tanks. The thunderous power of the bikes quaked the floor beneath my bare feet.

Mama scooted me by my shoulders out the back door of the kitchen, with my sister right behind me. "C'mon, girls." Her voice shook. "Stay out here until I call you in."

I shuddered. This wasn't like Mama.

Jami and I hurried back out to the backyard, and Mama tossed our flip-flops ahead of us into the dusty dirt. The eyesore of the neighborhood, our house on the hill stood out with a yard full of weeds and the occasional bloom of orange California poppies. The cascade of color down the side slope of the hill somehow made up for not having a nice lawn.

Mama didn't have time for gardening, though she picked apricots and managed her own roadside fruit stand growing up. Bikers stirred up clouds of dirt often. The rest of the houses on Savstrom Way were tended to with green lawns and flowering hedges. I suspected our neighbors didn't like us since they kept their curtains closed.

Mama did her best to keep us from getting caught in the middle of the biker parties, which took place day or night. I kept occupied in my own little world, away from the fighting, drinking, and drugs. Occasionally, our next-door neighbor, Johnny Simpson, would strike up a conversation with me through his bedroom window. Though a few years older than me, Johnny and I were the first born.

Jami and I attempted to cool ourselves in the yard. Thorny weeds speckled the dusty dirt. Jami grabbed the hose and placed the end in the soil, holding it there with great concentration so as not to make a huge mess. I adjusted the flow of water, glancing with hope for a sign of Johnny. "Careful," I said, "the water is hot." We collected our outside dishes from the wood crate Mama set near the back wall of the house. She filled it with old pots, bowls, kitchen gadgets, and utensils. We dug up the wet dirt with our large metal spoons, dumping it into the bowl. I offered the spoon to Jami. "Do you want to mix this time?" Nodding, Jami spooned the muddy mess. We let our imaginations run wild, pretending we were mixing up decadent chocolate-cream pies.

Jami jumped up and ran across the dusty yard to the red metal swing set that showed years of weather with rust spots here and there. I placed our creations on the back porch steps in the heat of the sun to bake when Jami called out, "Come push me."

The legs of the swing set wobbled and lifted from the ground when I pushed her too high. We usually ended up riding on the swinging teeter totter to balance the weight on the legs. Between giggles, we talked about how fun it would be to have a pool.

Our playtime ended when Mama summoned us from the back door, "Cherie! Jami! Time to come in."

Jami lowered her head with a heavy sigh. I helped her down from the swing. "Yeah, I know. Here we go." I tugged her arm. "C'mon. Mama will be mad if we track mud through the kitchen."

We headed to the garage to clean up, kicking up dirt the entire way. I sprayed our feet with the hot water from the hose. Loud music blared from the garage. Opening the garage door to the backyard a crack, I peered in. How were we supposed to get through there, with all those motorcycles and men?

Jami's hand clenched mine while doing the potty dance in her mud-spattered white top and red cotton shorts. "I gotta go!"

"Hold it." I shushed her.

A few bikers worked on their Harleys. One cleaned a gun and another adjusted big, heavy chains on his motorcycle. Most wore leather vests with patches. Hells Angels. Warlords. The same man who soaked our house with the garden hose unloaded guns from the trunk of Mama's car.

Still holding Jami's hand tight, I said, "Follow me. Quick!" My heart raced. While attempting to muffle the noise of the motorcycles with one hand, we made a beeline across the two-car garage to the opposite door into the house. I tried not to look at the bikers or get in their way.

Except for Little Joe, the President of the Warlords. He reminded me of James Dean with a dark Portuguese complexion and short black hair.

Little Joe claimed my mother as his ol' lady. If a biker liked a woman well enough to keep her as his personal property, he would take her as his ol' lady. It's a term of endearment. Now that Mama was Little Joe's ol' lady, he protected her like he would protect his guns and motorcycles. Being one's ol' lady is equivalent to wife status and greatly respected by the club brothers. Mama liked belonging to Little Joe. She didn't wear a 'property' patch indicating such, but even so, none of the club brothers ever messed with her out of respect for him. In fact, they were to protect her at all costs.

In some ways, knowing Little Joe was there helped.

The smell of grease, gas, and dirt from the bike motors penetrated the scent of laundry detergent from the washer. I grabbed two towels from the dryer to clean up with. Jami winced while pointing to a long, swordlike knife and heavy chain lying on a tire. Anxious, I urged her, "Don't look at them. C'mon." Jami quickly brushed past me and entered the house as soon as the door opened. Barely avoiding a stumble over the threshold, I quickly regained my composure and shut the door.

Mama raised her voice over the running bath water from down the hallway. "Bath time, girls. Hurry."

The sound of the bikes' motors filled our house, roaring and crackling, before gradually fading away as they rode off.

Chapter 3

W e were in and out of the tub, into our pajamas in a matter of minutes. Mama grabbed our coats from the hall closet. The sun was about to set, so I hoped we were going to the drive-in. But Mama wasn't bagging up popcorn. She loaded us up in the back seat of her 1962 Mercury Comet. The giant daisy decal covered a dent on the passenger door.

When we pulled into the parking lot of Kelly's Bar, an old notorious outlaw biker bar in downtown San Jose, I pulled Jami close to me. Frequent shootings took place at Kelly's Bar. I recalled the guns, chains, and other weapons in our garage. So, this is what the bikers were up to.

In the 1960s, the outlaw motorcycle gangs, a.k.a. the one percenters, were in a turf war in the San Francisco Bay Area. The Warlords of San Jose and the Oakland/San Jose chapters of Hells Angels prepared for the threat posed by the Gypsy Jokers—who wanted to claim San Jose as their territory. The Gypsy Jokers established their territory in San Francisco, carrying the reputation as the most notorious and violent motorcycle gang in both the U.S. and in Australia, with the exception of California. The Hells Angels held the most power in our neck of the woods.

Turf battles were intimately tied to efforts to build, maintain, or restore the reputation of the club members as well as the club name. Once a club established claim to a territory, it formed a local chapter of the club.

Outlaw motorcycle club patch holders wore a three-piece patch. The top piece, or top rocker, identified the name of the club. The bottom rocker identified the territory of the club and consisted of a country, state, or city and state such as Oakland, California. The center piece identified the official patch of the club. Usually made up of a custom graphic, this piece is considered sacred and protected by the club. A club member wearing a bottom rocker could not ride into the territory of a dominating club unless they first obtained approval of the established club in the area.

I figured all the commotion and weapons at our house were in preparation for what we were about to witness. The Gypsy Jokers would soon find out who San Jose belonged to.

Mama parked near the bar entrance. Little Joe stood outside the door with men wearing Hells Angels vests. He must have been looking for us because he walked up to Mama's window right away. He gestured for her to roll down her car window. Little Joe glanced toward the back seat. "Hey, girls!" He sounded surprised we were there. In a whisper, he asked, "What's up with that?" He leaned in to kiss her.

Mama touched his cheek and smiled. "They'll be fine. Rickie will make sure of it." She climbed out of the car, looking back at us over the leather seat. "Now, girls, I need you to stay right here. Rickie's going to sit with you. Mama's not going anywhere. I'll be right out here with Joe."

Jami leaned closer to me and laid her head on my arm.

The coolness of the leather seats chilled me through my pajamas. Disappointed, I nodded. "Okay, Mama." I gave her a confident look so she wouldn't know I'd rather be at the movies.

Rickie Rat, the Vice President of the Warlords, always told us funny stories. He opened the passenger door next to me and climbed into the back seat with us. The scent of motorcycle grease took over the inside of the car. His long wavy brown hair flowed into his beard. Rickie Ratt's big white teeth shone through his mustache. "Hey, look what I brought!" he said, holding up some children's books he'd read to us before. Jami reached for a book.

I didn't let Mama out of my sight. Jami scooted over to the other side of Rickie Rat so we both could see the pictures. I couldn't concentrate on listening to the story. I want to go home. Biting my fingernails, I tried again to spot Mama, but I could only see people walking into the bar. Each time a biker opened the door, the Rolling Stones blared from inside.

A few of the Warlords and Hells Angels stood against the trunk of our car, causing it to shake. My stomach tightened wondering what they were doing. I did not understand the brotherhood between the Warlords and the Hells Angels. I could attribute the connection to a Warlord's family member who rode with the Hells Angels. That's the impression they gave me when they ate at our dinner table.

In the distance, the throaty acceleration of motorcycles raced our way. Horns honked. I jumped up onto my knees for a better look. Bikers stormed out of the bar. I ducked down so they couldn't see me. Unable to contain my curiosity for more than a few heartbeats, I couldn't resist peeking again.

Rickie Rat patted my leg with his rough and calloused hand. "Sweetie, she's right there." He pointed toward the side of the building.

Okay, I see her now. I exhaled.

"C'mon, girls, let's finish our story." Rickie urged us with a shoulder-to-shoulder hug. "This is much better than what's going on out there." My curiosity intensified while I peeked out the passenger window from the backseat. Being at the bar felt wrong. Why couldn't Mama have gotten us a babysitter? Why did we have to be there?

A startling thump rocked the back of the car. Two bikers fell backward. One hit the other man in the face with a chain. I'd seen enough to know that when bikers fought, they wanted to kill each other.

My back stiffened, my grip tightening to the cool leather seat. Sliding down the seat to hide, I reached for Jami. "Where's my mama?" I cried. "I want to go home!" Jami's sobs mingled with mine.

Little Joe opened the driver's door and helped my mother by her shoulders into the car. He yelled for someone to come help. Mama cried when she started the car. "Babies, we're going home. Lie down." She took Rickie's hand over the back of the driver's seat. "Thank you, Rickie. They need you out there." Rickie patted my mother's hand, then hugged Jami and me.

Little Joe gave my mother a quick kiss through the driver's door window. He waved his arm toward the street. "Go now! Get them home!"

The screeching of cars caught my attention from the Monterey Highway, the main thoroughfare into downtown San Jose. I shrieked, "Mama, let's go! Fast!"

Mama drove toward the back of the building. I knelt, watching the war break out between the Warlords and Gypsy Jokers. Gunfire bursts made popping sounds. Men shouted and fought in the street. Three Hells Angels carried one of the Gypsy Jokers by his arms and legs and threw him into traffic. We tore out of there.

My breath sat on the edge of stilled lungs at the sight of it all. I wondered how much more my little heart could take.

Chapter 4

According to the *San Jose Mercury News*, Little Joe was the intended target, but Rickie Ratt died from a shotgun blast to the stomach. In a turf war, the only way to completely remove a rival club required taking out the president.

Right from the start, Little Joe and the Hells Angels had to run off the Gypsy Jokers. And that is what they did. Mama said Little Joe needed to lie low, so he didn't show up at our house for a bit.

Nightmares with gunshots and men fighting often woke me from my sleep. The sound of a car horn or a motorcycle roaring past our house shortened my breath. Hiding in my bedroom with my books helped take my mind off the fighting and gunshots.

With school about to start, Mama spent the next week shopping for school clothes for Jami and me. Fewer people were coming and going around our house, which I appreciated, though I missed Rickie Ratt and Little Joe. Thinking about moving from kindergarten across town to starting at the elementary school right around the corner from our house gave me something to look forward to. I didn't want to leave Miss Callahan. She deserved an award for World's Best Teacher. Two weeks before school started, Mama walked me to my new school office to look at the class assignments posted on the window. I hoped Miss Cook liked kids as much as Miss Callahan did.

Mama said having me in a school closer to our house would make things easier on her now that she had picked up extra shifts at the San Jose Airport. She often worked lunches and evenings as a cocktail server in the lounge. She looked fancy in her short red-and-black lace petticoat uniform. Our father used to take Jami and me to watch Mama work at the airport and would order us Shirley Temples. Mama said he always kept a close eye on her. People couldn't help but notice my mother, with her long, dark hair offset by her eyes as blue as the sky.

Whether Mama worked or not, our family of misfits played loud rock music with no regard for the neighbors. Van, the hang-around who blasted the biker with the hose in our living room, became a permanent fixture. He didn't do a thing aside from lying around on our round leopard print love seat. I didn't like the way he kept getting Mama to take pills called barbiturates. He ate them like candy. Something in my stomach felt strange about Van.

With so many people in and out of our house, Mama couldn't control the traffic of drugs. At times, jars of pills and rolls of cash lay at random places around the house. Guns were a different story. Pretty much everyone in the family packed a gun, including Mama and my grandmother. And part of her responsibility as Little Joe's ol' lady included supporting the club business, which meant running guns. She often buried them beneath the food she'd prepare for the bikers at the ranch.

I liked helping Mama in the kitchen even though I could barely reach the counter. We made sandwiches—peanut butter and jam and bologna with mayonnaise—with Nancy Sinatra playing on the record player. Mama nicknamed me 'Boots' after one of her songs: "These Boots Are Made for Walkin'."

One day after we made dozens of sandwiches on soft white bread and stuffed each one into its own baggie, she said, "Are you ready, Boots?"

I carefully folded the flap of the plastic baggie over the end of each sandwich. When the bikes roared up our street, Mama went out to the garage. Jami helped me pack the ice chest with the cokes and snacks. The big garage door slammed open, and the bikes rumbled into the garage. The whole house shook and made the glass grapes on top of the wood coffee table rattle.

I opened the door to the garage to let Mama know I finished packing the sandwiches. She and Rickie moved handguns and shot guns from a duffel bag into the trunk of Mama's car. Little Joe stood near his Harley and held out his arms. "Hey, kiddo! Come here and give me a hug!" I ran over, and he picked me up tight and swung me around. "What a good girl, helping us out." He kissed me on my cheek. He turned to Mama. "I thought we could drop the girls off with your mom before heading out there. It's best that nobody be here."

Mama nodded. "I'll call the babysitter and let her know there's been a change of plans."

Little Joe saw me watching him. "We're gonna do some target shootin,' baby girl." He smiled.

My heart sunk. I liked going to Little Joe's family ranch. We got to feed carrots and apples to the horses. I even learned how to pluck the pheasants in the giant metal laundry basin. They sure did stink! Mama and Little Joe said something about getting the 'tools' to the clubhouse. It seemed they were going to the Hells Angels clubhouse more often than before. Mama made it sound like they were having a good time, partying and shooting.

While we drove to Grandma Mary's, my mind shifted to the guns behind us in the trunk. Are we in danger? Mama had packed my small suitcase. She always reminded me of the time when I packed it all by myself and threatened to run away. I never left the porch that day. She let me stand out there for more than twenty minutes. I don't remember why at four years old I wanted to run away that night.

Grandma Mary knew of the outlaw life. She immigrated to the United States with my great-grandparents from Palermo, Sicily, during the prohibition era. My great-grandfather became a boot-legger for the mob. The outlaw mindset came naturally for the son of a Sicilian Mafia leader.

Mama once said my great-grandfather passed away months after she had me. My great-grandmother lived much longer. My mom's mother, Grandma Mary, lived with my great-grandparents. I never understood why I did not have a grandpa around. I learned much later that my grandparents divorced when Mama was my age. I thought it ironic that my father also lost his father before he turned five. Missing daddies apparently were common in our family.

Most of Mama's Sicilian side of the family now lived in Saratoga, California, a place much prettier than where we lived, less than an hour drive from our house. Grandma Mary's quiet neighborhood had no sidewalks, just lots of trees on both sides of the street. Sometimes the sun shined through the trees onto the street. The neighborhood, her yard, lush with green shrubs, colorful flowers, and fruit trees, reminded me of a movie.

Little Joe parked the car along the curb in front of my grand-mother's house. Mama thought it best for him to wait in the car since he hadn't yet met our family. I spotted Great-Grandma watering the yard. She raised her hand in a wave, with the garden hose never missing a beat. Her wavy shoulder-length hair, whitened over her eighty years, graciously framed the glow of her olive complexion. Her weathered yet delicate hands told of her passion for gardening, cooking, and cleaning. Rarely did I see her in anything besides her floral-printed apron, trimmed in lace, layered over her light cotton house dress. Her white shoes resembled those typically worn by nurses.

Mama helped Jami and me out of the car with our bags. Great-Grandma bent down, giving me big kisses on my cheek while she held my head in her hands. Mama said something to her in Sicilian as we walked up the porch. The sprawling rich, red flowering bougainvillea that framed the entrance to the house took me to a place I'd seen in a magazine.

Grandma Mary greeted us in the living room and said in her heavy Sicilian accent, "Hello, my little bambina." She pinched my cheeks hard, and I flinched and wrinkled my nose. I hated when she did that.

Her striking eyes were as green as a tropical forest and shoulder length hair she dyed black as coal. Most of the time, she wore a house dress. Today, she wore navy blue polyester slacks and a red blouse with house slippers and a feather duster in her hand. "Hello, Rosemary," Grandma said, barely smiling. She pointed Jami and me to the kitchen with the feather duster. "Come on in. You girls must be starving."

We were careful to not step off the path of clear heavy plastic that extended from the front door across the room. It kept the carpet, as well as the lush red velvet couches and chairs, clean and protected. Grandma never used the formal dining room area. Artifacts and collectible antiques from the early 1900s adorned the museum-like section of the house. Mama described how the tall Victorian floor lamp, with its massive carved claw feet and dome-shaped red silk lampshade trimmed in tiny glass fringed beads, triggered happy memories of her childhood on the family ranch where she'd grown up. She reminisced about searching for lucky pennies in the indoor wishing fountain so she could play the jukebox.

The stories behind each piece of antique furniture intrigued me, even at a young age. Some mirrors and picture frames were treasures salvaged from the 1906 San Francisco earthquake. I gravitated toward the floor lamp.

Grandma Mary barked from the doorway, "That's not for you to touch."

Great-Grandma's cooking filled the entire house with the smell of pizza, fresh-baked bread, and pasta dishes. Her kitchen lit up with natural light. Although my stomach growled, I was more thrilled to visit the fruit trees and flowers in her backyard. Mama pulled two chairs out for me and Jami. "Here, girls, sit up to the table."

For Sunday dinners, the whole family fit at the table. All fourteen of us, not counting five of us cousins at the kids' card table. Grandma prepared bowls of snacks and treats lined up from one end of the big table to the other. I enjoyed sitting at the grown-ups' table where I could see out the wall of windows out into the small orchard of trees in Grandma's backyard. I reached for a round powdery cookie as I took in the sweet fragrance of the large vase of fresh flowers from her garden, elegantly displayed in the center of Great-Grandma's old world Sicilian treats.

Even at an early age, I appreciated knowing I had roots. I looked forward to the evening but also feared whether Grandma Mary would go off on one of her drunken rants. Mama made certain that wouldn't happen this time. She hurried into the other room and said something to Grandma that I couldn't understand. Grandma Mary raised her voice back when Mama insisted on tossing any hidden bottles of brandy before she left. I could only make out something about not drinking. Mama told me Grandma nearly died while drinking and driving. My mother often referred to Grandma Mary as a walking miracle after running her car into a large tree. Though my grandmother landed in jail, she told Mama she'd gone to her country club.

Grandma Mary followed close behind as my mother inspected the obvious hiding places, ready to intercept her booze. "Minchia buttana!"

I knew my grandmother called my mother bad names. I heard it often, and Mama scolded me if I repeated the words.

Once the house inspection ended, my mother came to check on us before she left. Jami and I held our rare seats at the big table. Mama hugged us tight, kissing the top of Jami's head, then mine. "You girls behave for Grandma. I'll be back in the morning." She hurried out the old wooden screen door.

"Mangia! Mangia tutto!" Great-Grandma placed bowls of food in front of us.

Jami and I ate everything she served us, just like our great-grandmother insisted. Her noodles with spinach and lentils were one of my favorites.

When we were excused from the table, I requested permission from Grandma Mary to collect fruit like my Mama used to do. I took my garden basket from the white antique hutch. The creaking screen door slammed behind me. Careful not to disrupt the dried leaves between the brick pavers, I tiptoed my way along the winding path.

Figs were ripe for picking, the ones I could reach, anyway. I arranged them carefully in the basket. I knew they were perfect for Great Grandma's Sicilian fig cookies which were a highlight at our family dinners. I bit into the sweet, tender flesh of a fig when I walked back into the kitchen. Great-Grandma, smiling at me from the kitchen sink, tied up her apron.

Grandma Mary came in from the garage, carrying a box of vegetables. She set them down in the corner. "This is for your mother to take home when she gets here. What is she off doing now, anyway?"

I didn't know how to answer her or if I should say anything at all. I never knew how she would react. She sounded drunk again, her voice loud and agitated. She barked, "Well, the cat got your tongue?"

"I don't know, Grandma."

"And where's that loser daddy of yours?"

Not again. I hated it when she talked bad about my father. My mouth tightened. Tears welled in my eyes. I couldn't hold back any longer. Anger poured out. "Stop saying bad things about my daddy. I don't like when you call him names."

The tears wouldn't stop. I ran into the living room where Jami sat on the floor in front of the old Zenith television. I waited for Grandma to come after me, but she didn't. A storm of emotions raged within me. The rejection from my grandmother cast a heavy shadow, a painful wound etched deep in my tender heart. Her disapproval felt similar to a chilling wind that swept away the warmth of family love. And then, there was the haunting echo of my father's absence, an abandonment that left me adrift in a sea of loneliness. With my father leaving for my under-aged babysitter, I yearned for love, comfort, and belonging.

Not to be cast aside by my own grandmother because of the choices my parents made. I longed for the reassuring presence of a father who had become a distant echo in the recesses of my memories. The hurt and anger felt in that moment as my grandmother hurled her venomous comments knocked me to my knees, and the root of so much more to come.

Mama felt the venomous rejection from the family, too, when she became pregnant with me. Apparently, my great-grandfather was heartbroken when my mother, born Rosemary Lynn Street, gave up her life of affluence when she eloped into poverty with my father, Arthur LaLanne. Mama described how her grandfather and her own mother disowned her when she eloped. This all tied into me being born.

My heart, broken. My spirit, wounded. I grappled with grief, loss, unworthiness, and belonging all at the same time. Now we were the black sheep, the outcasts of the family. The ache of rejection and the void of abandonment intertwined, creating a symphony of heartbreak that would echo through the corridors of my childhood. Holding onto that narrative had a profound impact on how I perceived myself.

I didn't want to be here anymore.

Not ever.

Chapter 5

To my surprise, Mama picked us up late that night. I couldn't bear sleeping in my grandmother's house. Wearing my pj's, I ran to her at the front door and hugged her waist. Looking up, I asked, "Mama, do we get to go home now?"

She tried to smile behind a look of angst. "Yes, honey. Let me tell Grandma good night. Go get in the car."

Little Joe helped us into the back seat. When he finished, Mama slid across the front seat, close to him. I needed to tell her and finally mustered up courage to speak. "I don't want to spend the night here again, Mama. Grandma's mean." I tugged at my pajamas.

Mama reached back over the leather seat and held my hand. "Grandma's sick, honey. Don't worry." She smiled in an effort to comfort me. "We'll be home soon."

I did my best to ignore the conversation between my mother and Little Joe. Having to deal with my grandmother was already too much for me. Regardless, I wanted to know what I could expect at home.

Little Joe talked about more retaliation from the Gypsy Jokers. Mama described sitting up at the top of the Hells Angel's watchtower with Little Joe and the club brothers, locked and loaded, getting high and looking out for rival clubs. Because that's what family did. The few remaining Warlords became members of the Hells Angels after the ambush at Kelly's Bar. He lowered his voice, but I could hear Little Joe telling my mother that the war hadn't ended yet. He said the Angels will take care of it.

Things changed drastically almost immediately. We didn't see Little Joe much after that night. Mama lost many of her close friends, and the Jokers kept coming around looking for the Warlords. Every now and then, I overheard Mama crying on the phone. Ultimately, Little Joe told her she was better off without him. I know Mama loved Little Joe deeply, because she cried often. I cried too. I loved and trusted him enough to be our new daddy.

Important men in uniforms began showing up at our house looking for Little Joe. I later found out that he went AWOL from the Army. The federal government doesn't like soldiers to go absent without official leave.

Van, the hang-around assigned to protect us in Little Joe's absence, became our protector. His shorter muscular frame and clean-cut appearance did not quite match up to the image of a burly biker. But Little Joe trusted Van. In the aftermath of the biker wars, the Gypsy Jokers continued their retaliation, like Little Joe warned. Van suggested to my mother that we leave our house until things calmed down.

Over time, Van became more than a friend to my mother. Mama learned of Van's recent motorcycle accident and the aftereffects of his traumatic brain injury. He relied on barbiturates and a variety of drugs to help with seizures.

Mama trusted him. She didn't have a choice. That warning in my stomach about him subsided. Our neighbor, Arlene, encouraged my mother to listen to Van. As Mama's best friend, she promised to watch over our house for the next few months. Next thing I knew, we were packed up and out of there. Van seemed like someone I could trust. After all, he wanted to protect us, and he invited us to his house on the other side of town, about thirty minutes away.

Van's parents welcomed us and treated us like their own grand-children. We stayed in a small pool house in the backyard of their home. Jami and I slept in a small area with a twin bed. Mama and Van slept in their own room in the main house. The plans for the new school year changed again. At least I would continue attending Miss Callahan's school for the time being. But I wasn't sure how I felt about our circumstances. I did miss our house, but not the bikers.

Van's two teenage sisters were beautiful, and they twirled batons and marched in parades. The sisters treated Jami and me like family and invited us into their bedroom where they proudly showed off their shelves of trophies from their baton twirling tournaments. Their parents bought Jami and me batons of our own. I wanted to learn how to throw the baton way up in the air and spin around a bunch of times before catching it. I practiced as often as I could, but I could never get the hang of it.

Like Grandma Mary's neighborhood, their street was quiet with overgrown trees and vibrant flowers, but the yards were even more beautiful. Van's parents had an aboveground pool in their backyard and often invited guests over for dinner and card games. I loved having a pool to play in. Van taught me how to swim by repeatedly throwing me into the deep end. I thought I would drown.

After several months of living there, Van and Mama decided to get married. My mother knew how badly I needed a father. After all, she saw I had already adopted the use of Van's last name on my school paper. And since my father landed in prison, I saw no hope of his return. I dreamed of becoming a lawyer when I grew up so I could keep him out of jail. I needed a father, and if it wasn't my birth father or Little Joe, it must be Van. Throughout this story, to avoid confusion, I'll always refer to him as Van.

By the time winter was over, Van thought it was safe to move back to the house on the hill. Settling back into our familiar surroundings with our new dad gave me a sense of security. I'd be starting school again with my first-grade teacher, Miss Cook. Jami started kindergarten.

Van played with us often, though it felt strange when he wanted us to drink beer and smoke marijuana to help us sleep. I didn't try it, but Jami did. One night, Van giggled with Jami on her bed. His behavior felt unsettling and marked the beginning of much more to come. Van's bullying and sudden bursts of rage became the norm shortly after he married my mother. His unstable mental health, coupled with an addiction to narcotics, unleashed unpredictable violence. Why the Warlords called upon him to do their dirty work was clear.

Nobody, including my mother, showed moral judgment by having Van around Jami and me. If any of us sassed Van, we would be at the mercy of his unrelenting fury. He kept his brown leather strap out in the open as a constant reminder. Van treated us differently while Mama worked nights. However, she was always at home in the mornings. If Mama came home from work later than expected, all hell broke loose.

One night, Jami and I did not come quickly enough when Van called for us from the living room. He stormed into our bedroom with the fierceness of a rabid animal. He waved the leather strap and demanded we lean up against the ladder on our bunk bed. I choked down my tears. Jami's tears flowed while catching her breath between sobs. We gripped the ladder, hiding our faces with our eyes squeezed shut. I touched Jami's hand. He took turns beating us until the back of our legs showed welts. First me, then Jami. Back and forth. During breakfast the next morning, a prayer covered up the torment.

I wanted Little Joe for our stepfather, not Van. Little Joe would never hurt us. I found myself in yet another state of confusion. Why would Van hurt us when he was told to protect us? How could he betray my mother when he told her he loved her? I thought he loved my mother. Loved us. First, my father left with our babysitter. Now Little Joe left us with this monster. I'll never understand why my mother didn't insist on packing up and staying with Little Joe. He must have known life would only become harder on us.

Mama and Van often spoke of Little Joe, wondering whatever happened to him. The rest of the surviving Warlords were welcomed into the Hells Angels as patch holders. Some died while others went to prison. The headlines sent some into hiding, while Mama's favorite brothers from the Hells Angels thought it best to lie low and not attract more attention. The thought of Little Joe and Rickie Rat made me cry. Why didn't some Hells Angels check on us to make sure we were okay? They thought Van would take good care of us.

In third grade, I became fascinated with horses. One day after school, while watching cartoons in the living room, Van asked me, "How would you like to go horseback riding this weekend?" He held something behind his back. "Just you and me."

I squealed, bouncing up and down on the couch. "Yay! Do I get to ride my own horse now?"

Van held up a small brown leather vest, turning it around to show the laces up the sides and silver conchas on the front. "Yes, honey. We're going on a trail ride. Your mama even made you a leather vest.

You'll be a real cowgirl." I loved the smell of leather and Mama cut it to fit perfectly.

Van checked us in at the nearby horse-riding stables. He picked out the perfect size horse for me with big brown and white spots. His horse stood much taller. Van kept hold of the leather reins of my horse during our hour-long dusty trail ride. After, we made our way across the parking lot to the van. I stood by the passenger door, eager to get out of the heat.

Van gave me a boost into the front seat and climbed onto the mattress in the back of the van. He opened the lid of the ice chest filled with drinks.

"Come on back here and cool off for a few minutes." He patted the mattress he used for overnight fishing trips and handed me a can of soda. He lay back, and I sat on the edge of the mattress with my cool drink. We talked about the horses.

"Lie back," he said, "and let's grab a quick nap. I'm tired."

I couldn't nap, but I laid back anyway and waited for him to fall asleep. Then he touched my hair. And Van didn't stop there. I squirmed and moved my head from side to side. "Stop it!" I tried to yell, but he covered my mouth.

He stopped and moved to the driver's seat. "Get up here and get buckled in. You're not going to say anything about that."

I cried silently on the drive home. I couldn't say a word to anyone or there would be hell to pay by either me, my sister, or Mama. Any future fun activities with Van came at a similar price. He taught me to lie to my mother to protect her. My silence lessened my beatings. All the while, Van mastered the charade of a caring father with trips to the park, the zoo, and ice cream runs while instilling fear.

The more I could do away from the house, the better. Mama signed me up for Brownies, which provided a huge reprieve. Weekly troop meetings gave me a safe place away from Van, at least for a while.

When I showed an interest in music, my parents took me to a guitar studio and let me pick out a fancy steel slide guitar. The store owner called it a Hawaiian guitar. Van usually drove me to my private guitar lessons. I became so good at playing Hawaiian-sounding music that my third-grade teacher arranged for me to play at the school assembly.

Playing in front of all those people frightened me. My teacher gave me an achievement award for good grades and a small plastic trophy for playing guitar in front of the entire school. Mama doted on me in front of everyone.

As Mama's number one, she often put me in charge of Jami, reminding me to make sure nothing happened to her. I always worked hard for Mama's approval by doing my chores and eating all the food on the table. She began handing me the money so I could chase down the ice cream truck. When Jami and I did get in trouble, Mama came down harder on Jami. Getting Jami to behave was more difficult for Mama.

Keeping Jami and me occupied with Van and his dog training business helped us both stay out of trouble. My parents loved dogs and opened an obedience and protection training school. Van trained the dogs with German commands. That was so the dogs wouldn't listen to strangers' English commands.

So many people signed up for his weekend workshops that Van held classes at the school playground or at the park. He trained dogs to listen to their owners. That included teaching the dogs not to attack cats. When he put our kitty in a cage and set it inside the circle of dogs, I thought they would eat my cat. Thank goodness they didn't.

After that, I gave our kitty extra hugs. And I wished Van would use someone else's pet.

One day we met at the park with close to twelve police dogs and their owners. In this class, Van taught the dogs how to attack bad guys. Van volunteered us as his assistants. After directing the owners to line up facing the trees, he slid his arm into the big, heavy sleeve made of burlap and put a scary mask over his face. He hid in the trees and whistled for us. We didn't know what to expect. We took our cue and held hands while we walked slowly on the path.

The dog's owner commanded with authority, "Achtung." That meant, "Watch."

Van jumped out of the trees and grabbed us, yelling.

The owner continued to shout, "Fass! Fass!"

The dog listened to the command to attack and ran at us. My sister and I ran when the dog jumped at Van. It tried to kill him as it tore at the burlap sleeve with its sharp teeth. Jami and I held on to each other. We watched them struggle and wrestle for what seemed forever. Van enjoyed fighting the dogs, but it scared me. I'd never seen something so vicious. I didn't like what I saw in Van either.

Finally, the dog's owner called the dog off. "Aus!"

After several hours, Van trained the last dog, and we went home. When mom left for work, the lingering smell of pot roast filled the house. After seeing Van acting so mean with the dogs and all, I wished Mama didn't have to work.

He kissed Mama goodbye and called us to the dinner table. We said our daily prayer over dinner: "God is great. God is good. Let us thank Him for our food. Amen."

Even Jami ate everything on her plate. We didn't have much choice when Van watched us.

Chapter 6

After dinner, Van left us in the living room while he took a shower. I wanted to grab my sister and run and hide when the shower stopped running. Van called from the bedroom, "Hey, can you bring me a towel?"

My voice cracked and my throat nearly closed shut. "The towels are right there. You can reach them." I clenched my teeth. I'm not going back there. He doesn't have any clothes on.

Jami gasped, and she began to tremble. Talking back must have seemed crazy to her.

Van called again. "Jami, can you get Daddy a towel?"

Jami looked at me for approval, and I shook my head. "You don't have to go back there. Stay here."

I remembered Mama telling me to make sure nothing happened to Jami. At five years old, she needed her big sister. I held her hand to keep her next to me. Van stood at the end of the hallway, holding a bath towel loosely around his waist. He gestured to Jami to get up. "Come here. I want you to see how cute the dogs are playing in the backyard."

Jami knew if she did not go with him, it would only make things worse. I bit my bottom lip and shook my head. Why didn't I go get the stupid towel? Van's attempt at creating a façade of laughter did not mask my sister's cries. So much for protecting her. How would I explain to Mama that I couldn't keep Van from hurting Jami?

A few days later, I mustered up enough courage to tell my mother. I figured if I told her, Van would leave and never touch us again. Catching her at the right time meant I had to make sure Van wasn't around. He usually slept in later in the mornings when Mama was up getting us ready for school. At breakfast, I asked her if she could stay home from work that night. When she asked why, I told her Van had been touching us in our private parts. I took a deep breath and chose my words carefully. "Mama, he hurt Jami bad. He locked her in your bathroom with him." I tried to hold back my tears so I could speak. "She kept screaming, Mama. There was nothing I could do."

My mother's averted gaze conveyed her desire to reject the unwelcome truth. After a few seconds, she affirmed my courage. "You did good, honey."

I didn't want Van to hurt Mama if she got mad at him. It didn't matter, anyway. Nothing changed.

After that night, Jami turned mean and kept fighting with me. Perhaps she was mad about Mama saying she wasn't supposed to be born. I remembered her saying something about wanting an abortion. I didn't understand. Why would Mama say things like that?

Van's affection for Jami seemed to make Mama jealous. Jami's constant tantrums and health issues also took its toll on my mother. We made weekly trips to see the doctor. Jami developed allergies to most everything, including dog hair and dust, which were plentiful at our house. Her food allergies also worsened, and I heard Mama talking on the phone about Jami being out of control.

The doctor put Jami on medication to calm her, but it didn't help. Mama never told the doctor about Van hurting Jami so terribly.

Nobody knew the extent of how often he molested her. I only knew my sister needed more than a visit to the doctor. The guilt and anger from that night haunted my mind. Why didn't I do something? I'm supposed to protect her!

One morning from my bedroom, I overheard Mama on the kitchen phone. In a whispered voice, she told my Aunt June, my father's sister-in-law, all about her struggles with Jami. She made plans for Jami to go live with her and my Uncle Mick for a while. A lump formed in my throat. Good thing, because I wanted to yell at my mother to send Van away instead of Jami.

I spent more time with my friends after Jami moved. Johnny and David, the two brothers next door, were always alone too. Their mom worked in her hair salon and went out at night. They weren't allowed to leave the front yard most of the time. As a sixth grader, Johnny became like a big brother to me. I always wanted a big brother, so the bullies wouldn't bother me.

Mom told me I would marry Johnny one day. She arranged for Jami to come home for the weekend so we could go to the school magic show together. Mama dressed Jami and me like we were going out on a date with the Simpson boys. I felt embarrassed getting all dressed up in my cousin's rich clothes for a magic show. And Johnny was like my big brother. Mama always made things fun, but I wished she hadn't made it feel weird. Would my friends also think I was on some sort of date with a sixth-grade boy? I wondered what my third-grade teacher would think.

The next day, Mama broke the news that she was pregnant. All I wondered was if Van would hurt him the same way he had us. But, as my little brother grew into a toddler, I watched him most of the time. Because of Van's new job at a flea market across town, he was not at home as much. He hadn't worked since he started training dogs. The maintenance job required us to live on the property, about an hour away. We moved out of our house and Mama boarded the place up. She pulled me out of my school and away from all my friends. Mama explained we were in for a new adventure, but I'd had enough changes in my life.

My new bedroom really wasn't a bedroom. The building we lived in extended from the offices and concession areas of the flea market. Wooden posts divided the long white room where the old concession booths once were. The wooden panel on the wall opened like a window so customers could walk up to order their food. Van put a mattress on the floor for me in there. It smelled old.

The flea market opened for business on Saturday mornings. This gave me something to look forward to all week. Plus, I was free to visit the ponies and roam the flea market grounds when they were closed to the public. I loved waking early to the smell of the fresh-baked French bread from the bakery concession stand. I looked forward to free homemade bread, warm from the oven, with a package of Italian salami sliced up thin for us. The sweet Italian lady who ran the bakery made the best bread and butter pickles too.

One weekend, after the gates closed behind the last group of vendors, Mama surprised us with her yummy meatloaf. Van always took care of chores at closing time. He hurried to finish dinner and rinsed out his glass in the kitchen sink. "C'mon, sweetie," he said to me. "Finish your dinner. You can help me clean out the shed before it gets dark."

I gulped down the last bite of mashed potatoes. "Okay." I didn't dare argue with him about wanting to stay in and practice my violin. I also figured Mama could use the silence.

Van drove a golf cart to haul tools around the four-hundred-acre property, which the owners also used for storage and hunting. When I climbed into the golf cart, Van handed me a blanket. "Here. It might get cold out there." I folded it across my lap.

The shed held nothing more than a bunch of metal toolboxes and equipment he used to clear the brush away from the buildings.

His manipulation, too obvious, I looked around. "So, what are we cleaning up?"

"Oh, I need to fix a couple of boards that came loose. You can see them around back." He pointed out the side door.

I tensed and tried to figure out how I could run straight home. But then Mama would know. "I'll wait here while you fix the boards."

"It's getting dark." He walked over to me with the blanket.

The only thing I remember after that was fighting him off. He stopped when I threatened to scream. I didn't want to get back in that dumb golf cart with him, but I did. I sat with my hands clasped under the blanket. I need to get home. Straighten up. Mama can't know. I wanted to die.

I'd steer clear of those hidden areas, but he'd always trick me into thinking we were gonna have a good time. I hated my breasts showed more and I needed a bra before turning ten years old. Van teased me about it so much that I began hiding them with my long hair.

Then Mama received a phone call from my father. He wanted to visit now that he'd been released from prison. I bounced up and down with a squeal and clenched my fists with excitement. Pure joy filled my cheeks. My real father? He'll help me. I just knew it.

Sure enough, he started coming around with his girlfriend. Mama, Van, my father, and his girlfriend all became friends. My father hunted pheasant and jack rabbit on the property with Van. I didn't know which one to call Daddy and I didn't want to hurt anyone's feelings. I wondered if my father thought I didn't love him anymore.

Watching my father laugh at Van's hunting stories disgusted me. How could I tell him about Van hurting Jami and me? He might kill him if he knew. How on earth could Mama not see what was going on with me if she knew what Van did to Jami? I couldn't understand how she could always leave me alone with Van, knowing what a monster he was.

I eventually thought it best not to say anything to anyone. I feared Mama would send me away like she did Jami. I didn't want to leave the flea market or Mama. I loved the daily adventures, such as visiting the lady who ran the pony rides. She boarded the ponies in the arena and gave us permission to play with them when she was not there.

My Grandpa Don came to visit from Washington too. I had not seen my grandpa since I was a baby, when my parents moved back to California from Washington. I met my mother's little sister, Dona, who was only three years older than me. Though she was my aunt, Dona and I became best friends overnight. I looked forward to Grandpa driving her over from their hotel. We enjoyed hanging around the regulars who came to sell their stuff every weekend. The vendors often gave us little things they couldn't sell.

One day, I saw a typewriter for sale in one building. I ran through the commercial kitchen into the living room which someone had converted from an office space. Mama sat on the carpet with my baby brother. Robert had finally learned to walk. In a blink of an eye, my little blond-haired, blue-eyed brother seemed to go from crawling to running.

With a grin ear to ear, I squealed, "Mama. Mama. I found the same typewriter Mrs. Taylor had in her classroom. It's only twenty-five dollars."

We couldn't afford it, but Santa could. Even with Van losing his maintenance job and housing at the flea market, we still enjoyed Christmas. Moving back into our house on the hill was the best Christmas present ever. Mama rolled out my typewriter on a metal stand with wheels. It looked exactly like the one I saw at the flea market.

I began getting in trouble for fighting boys at school. I hated it when boys bullied my girlfriends. And I hated Van and how he bullied me. He staged one of his worst scenes on a family Thanksgiving at our house. We usually spent Thanksgiving at Grandma Mary's house, then with Van's parents. This year, since Jami had returned from living with Aunt June, Mama wanted to cook Thanksgiving dinner at home.

Van chose not to sit at head of the table. When he sat next to me, my neck tightened. I folded my hands in my lap and tried not to look nervous. I said grace, the same one we had said for years.

Van's face turned red. "Pass me the salt." His voice, tense.

He could have reached it himself, but I passed it to him anyway. He started poking my bare leg with his fork.

I winced and jerked my leg, then snapped at Van. "Stop it."

He sprung out of his chair, grabbed me by my neck with his rough hand and lifted me from my chair. He stumbled and the table fell over with a loud thud. Mama's Thanksgiving dinner crashed to the floor. Jami screamed. He carried me across the kitchen while gripping my neck, pinned me against the wall, banged my head, and squeezed my throat. I couldn't breathe.

Van's veins bulged from his neck. "Don't you ever talk back to me, young lady. Do you understand?"

Mama scrambled from the mess on the floor. She pounded on Van's back, screaming with fear. "Let go of my daughter." She reached for me, and continued yelling.

He loosened his grip and lowered me to the floor.

Coughing to get air, I ran to the bathroom.

Thanksgiving dinner ruined, the fighting between my mother and Van went on all night.

I sensed she feared him more than I did.

Chapter 7

Things were different between me and Jami now. Mama treated me as her favorite and Jami hated me for it. We fought nearly every day. One day Jami tried to stab me with a dinner knife, so I threw my mother's big gold glass table lamp at her. She dropped the knife and went running out the front door to tell the neighbor. I locked her out of the house and called Mama at work. Calling Mama at work became a habit.

As if things weren't bad enough, Mama became obsessed with the occult. She read tarot cards after visiting a psychic. She liked to have her cards read and to hear about her future, and dabbled with what she called black magic.

Mama shared all about her new hobby with my Aunt Dona. Having Dona around felt like having a big sister. Grandpa could no longer afford to stay in a hotel, and he needed help to get settled after his recent release from prison. So, my mother let them have Jami's bedroom.

Grandpa moved in with Dona and her younger brother, Barry, who was only a year older than me. They enrolled in our school, Samuel E. Stipe, which was around the corner from our house. When my friends discovered my aunt and uncle were classmates, they were shocked.

Having a sixth-grade aunt as a fourth grader added excitement to life. Dona introduced me to wearing makeup, shaving my legs, and wearing clothes that made me look older. I suddenly had a big sister who nobody messed with which meant they did not mess with me. Hanging out with Dona gave me more freedom, too. We loved taking the bus to the mall across town. Dona went boy crazy, though. And Van liked her too. He stared at her breasts, which were more developed than any sixth grader I'd ever seen. Many days I hoped mine wouldn't get that big.

I also knew I needed to warn her to stay away from him. The fighter in me wanted to stand up for those who would, or could, not stand up for themselves. In addition to protecting my sister, I instinctively protected my girlfriends at school and now my aunt from bullies.

Grandpa Don treated Dona like a princess. Mama too, from the stories they reminisced about at the dinner table. His wild stories about his life sounded like scenes straight from crazy action movies. Sometimes I didn't believe him, like when he ran after a car on fire. When Mama described Grandpa as a great storyteller, I thought he wrote fairy tales. Among my grandfather's stories, the ones with Elvis Presley and his crew were the most thrilling. His claim that we were cousins of Elvis seemed so far-fetched. Mom proved my assumptions wrong when she showed me the check she received from the Presley Family Trust. Our share amounted to less than one hundred dollars. We laughed about being on the bottom rung. I never would have guessed that I would be related to a celebrity, let alone the King of Rock 'n Roll himself.

Discovering some of my grandfather's exploits, I understood he was not to be underestimated. I witnessed that firsthand within a few months of him living with us. Mama had caught Van in bed with

Dona. Jami and I were in our bedroom when the screaming ensued. I had to see what was happening and stepped into the hall. Mama cussed at Van and hit him with her fists. Grandpa hurried from the living room to see what was going on. That's all it took. Grandpa pulled my mom off of Van by her shoulders. "Lynnie, get the girls and stay out of the way." She grabbed us tight on each side and we clung to each other while sitting on the edge of her bed.

I saw Van fall backward onto the floor in the hallway when Grandpa shoved him out of the guest bedroom. Grandpa grabbed his shotgun and aimed it at Van. "Get out of here! You're never touching my family again!" Grandpa threw in few cuss words too. Van crawled backward to get away, shielding his face with his hand. "Don, don't shoot!" He stood there, his eyes aimed at me in desperation, and begged. "Girls, don't you want to come with Daddy?"

Jami and I clung to our mother, crying and afraid. Mama held us tighter. I hid my face in her arm. Her body trembled. Deep down inside, I wanted Grandpa to shoot him. I hid my eyes to keep from watching it happen.

Jami sobbed harder and screamed. "No, Mama! Don't make us go with him!"

This man who claimed to be our daddy, who continually bullied and intimidated us into doing exactly what he said, no longer held power over us. We had Grandpa to thank for that. I reached forward and slammed my mother's bedroom door shut. I stood, screaming as loud as I could through the door. "We're staying with Mama!"

Grandpa made sure Van left the house. My Aunt Dona, in tears, lay on her bed. I tried to warn her. Fortunately, he did not hurt her, thanks to Grandpa showing up when he did. I looked to my grandpa as a hero after running Van off. I wasn't convinced we were truly rid of him since he was still alive. But God did answer our prayers by finally removing him from our lives.

After Van left, my grandfather found his own apartment for him, Dona, and Barry and Dave, another one of my mom's half-brothers. Dona preferred to hang out at our house instead of with an apartment full of guys. I think she had more privacy with us and did not have to worry about her brothers or dad snooping around in her diary at my house. She even gave me one of her additional diaries, so I started keeping one at twelve years old.

One of my first entries read:

Dear diary, I'm in love with Ralphie. I hope he kisses me soon.
If he doesn't, I'll put my arm around Billy.
I'm calling my mama "Mom" from now on. I'm not a little girl anymore.
She better not flirt with Billy. I'll be so mad at her. Good night!

My daily entry usually included the list of boys I'd thought of that day. Some pages contained the names of up to six boys. When Mom went out on a date, often with different men, sneaking out at night to rendezvous with guys became my norm. Age didn't matter. My mom and I went boy crazy together. She loved the bad boys, and so did I.

Mom tried to tell me eighteen-year-olds were off-limits. That didn't seem fair because they weren't off-limits for her or her sister. Aunt Dona introduced me to all the older boys who came over to our house to party with her and Mom. The guys enjoyed flirting with me, and I loved the attention.

Dona and my mom met some guys, two brothers and their cousin, who began hanging out at our house. I could not resist eighteen-year-old Roger's clean cut 'greaser' look from the fifties. Plus, he drove a '57 Chevy.

Full of charm and all the compliments a young girl could handle, Roger swept me off my feet in an instant. My hormones fired on all cylinders with intense passion. Our weekly rendezvous escalated into losing my virginity to him.

A couple of weeks later, Roger took me to his cousin's house. We were only supposed to swing by the mobile home park to pick something up real quick. After fifteen minutes, Roger stepped out of the trailer and waved from the porch steps for me to get out of the car.

Oblivious to what I'd gotten myself into, I agreed to go inside to meet his cousin, Raymond. Only there were several other older men there. They took turns raping me. Though the alcohol and pot laced with angel dust kept me from remembering little about the details from that night, I do recall begging each of the men not to beat me.

Roger didn't come around again after my mom found out what had happened. She also forced me to take a pregnancy test.

I returned to spending my weekends going to Frontier Village, an amusement park with shootout reenactments, stagecoach rides, and a haunted mine. Mom bought Jami and me a season pass every year for the past three years. She would cut us loose when she dropped us off at the front gate. That was her opportunity to do her own thing. I appreciated that she grasped the fact I no longer needed a babysitter.

When I became the babysitter, that was a whole different story. Especially one Saturday morning when Mom left early for a day at the beach with a girlfriend from work. I got stuck babysitting Bobby and Jami. Jami's friend, Leticia, slept over and they were outside, hanging out in a fort they built along the side yard beneath my bedroom window.

I occupied my little brother with a book on our black leather couch when a loud boom shook the whole side of the house. I nearly fell to the ground. The shattering of glass from the explosion sounded as if our windows blew out. "What the heck?" I pulled back the heavy gold-and-black drapery from the living room window. Big puffs of smoke billowed up and into the house.

Our neighbor from next door yelled, "Fire! Get out! Fire!"

The tips of flames climbed up the side of the house.

Bobby ran over to me, crying, and clung to my leg.

I couldn't see my sister through the smoke. "Jami, are you okay?"

She cried from the front porch; her voice muffled by the sound of choking coughs. "Yes, we're fine."

Neighbors ran to our rescue and hurried us out of the house to safety. We huddled together in the driveway. The smoke grew thicker while the flames consumed the side of our house. Watching the flames engulf the roof line of my bedroom filled me with terror. "Our house can't burn down," I yelled. "Mom's going to kill us when she gets home."

One neighbor used his garden hose to spray water up the sloped side of our yard, quenching the flames and wet down the dried weeds. The fire department arrived within minutes. Wide-eyed and trembling, I kept Jami and Bobby at a safe distance while we witnessed the frenzy of the firefighters pulling huge firehoses from the truck. My eyes darted around the team of heroes battling the blaze. "Oh my God, please save our house. Please!"

Jami held her hands to her face, sobbing. Her friend rushed off to get home. Firefighters took an ax to my bedroom wall to ensure the fire no longer burned inside the walls.

When Mom pulled up to the house, she ran to us in absolute disbelief. My mother looked to me first for answers. I told her all I knew was there was an explosion of glass and flames from Jami's fort. My sister stood with her head hung in fear and shame. She mumbled, "We were smoking, Mama. I'm sorry." Jami broke down in uncontrollable tears, probably more from fear than anything else. Mom yelled at her for thinking she could smoke cigarettes at age ten.

Not long after, Mom sent Jami to her room for mouthing off. Mom overheard Jami tell Leticia she wanted to live with our father. That sealed it. Mom didn't hesitate to call him. "Art, I have never asked you for anything. But right now, your daughter needs you. She wants to come live with you."

Jami didn't want to go, but it was too late now. Our father arrived from Antioch within a couple of hours to pick her up. Mom was quick to send my sister away again. She did not know how to change or manage my sister's behavior. Jami cried with confusion and sorrow. My sister asked for this, but she didn't mean it. Mom didn't care. Jami and I experienced heartbreak that I will never forget.

Mom relied on me to take care of Bobby, who was just about to start kindergarten. When I could get out of the house, I went to Grandpa's to hang out with Dona. I could go anywhere with her. My mom finally let me go out again after what happened with Roger. And she let me go out with Dona. One weekend, we took the bus to the mall and shop for makeup and new bellbottom Levi's.

Our plan included flirting with guys at the county fair that night. We walked to the bus stop only a couple city blocks from Grandpa's downtown apartment. Cars honked when they drove past us while we walked along the busy street. They startled me enough to walk faster. Men whistled and hollered at Dona. She bore the same striking features as my mom, with dark-brown hair and big blue eyes.

Some slowed to get a closer look. That made me nervous, so I ran to the bushes to hide when a car came too close. Dona seemed to enjoy the attention and would even smile and say hi back to them.

"Get over here, silly," she said after one car pulled away. "There's nothing to be afraid of."

We were at the bus stop when the bus passed us by. It didn't even stop at the bus stop ahead of us.

"What's up with that?" I asked. "He kept going!"

Another car slowed and pulled to the curb ahead of us. I had a feeling that Dona might recognize the person in the car as she walked towards them ahead of me.

Looking behind for me, she waved her hand at me to hurry up. "C'mon. I know these dudes. They'll give us a ride."

Two guys sat inside the old, white Impala. The driver was a White guy with rumpled, light-brown hair. The passenger was a towering Black man with a massive afro. His height made it difficult to look out the passenger window. Dona stood at his passenger door, leaning in.

I walked a little closer to the car. The guy in the passenger seat stared down Dona's top. I looked into the back-seat window. When I saw a knife, it triggered memories of the bikers preparing for war. I pictured our stepfather with his homemade leather knife sheath strapped to his leg.

I panicked and took off running toward the apartment. "Dona, let's go!"

"What are you doing?" Dona screamed and chased after me. "Get back here!"

I ran into the bushes again. Through the leaves, I saw the car pull away. I exhaled. What a relief. They would have killed us. She's crazy. I want to go home.

With a mixture of fear and anguish, I screamed, tears welling up in my eyes. "Don't ever do that to me again!"

"Nothing happened," she scolded. "Don't you ever run from me again, do you hear? We have to stick together."

"I saw a knife!"

I flashed back to the words I'd read in my Hansel and Gretel fairy tale: God will not forsake us. I did not understand the word 'forsake.' But I knew Hansel wanted to assure his little sister God would not let them die. I couldn't help but wonder if God saved us from harm.

Keeping my grades up always remained important to me, though it didn't take much for me to ace my tests. I also didn't mind helping my new girlfriends when they asked me to do their homework. I kept my teacher's pet status going into junior high school, except for the teachers who gave me attitude. I turned defiant and became known as a fighter.

The leader of a Mexican girls' gang tried recruiting me at the start of my seventh-grade year. That I wasn't Mexican surprised her. For some reason, as a White girl, they respected me. They assured me that no matter what, I could count on them to have my back.

I made a couple of new friends at school and hung out at their houses as much as I could. Kathleen and Brandy quickly became like sisters to me. They enjoyed hanging out at my house because we could party there. Mom still believed I could do no wrong, so I couldn't disappoint her by letting the cat out of the bag that I smoked pot. If she knew, she would put a stop to my going out with Dona.

My circle of friends at school were labeled stoners. We thought we were the cool kids. I cut class to hang out with all the new friends. One time, Mom found out and knocked me to the floor with one blow to my head. I attempted to block her arms with my feet while she relentlessly came towards me, even though I was lying on the floor. That only infuriated her more.

That ended my time of being the perfect daughter. So, I did what I learned from her—seeking guys who claimed girls as their possessions. This trait seemed to flow through our family bloodline. Hopping on the back of a Harley while crossing the street became a thing for me. I wanted to be a biker's ol' lady, like my mother.

Grandma Mary called our house often, asking of Mom's whereabouts and calling her many awful names. She kept calling, even knowing Mom wasn't home. She wouldn't listen when I asked her to stop talking so badly about my mother. The calls came all hours of the night when Mom worked, so I unplugged the phone. I never understood how she could talk so awful about her own daughter.

Mom talked often about her years attending Catholic school. After she caught me cutting school, she threatened me. She'd say things like, "If you keep it up, I'll ship you off to Catholic school. The nuns can deal with you."

I wondered if God is good, why does she threaten me with religion? I longed for goodness in people. I sensed it in the way I felt when I went to Kathleen's house. Her parents were Jehovah's Witnesses and were kind. The family across the street were Mormon and acted the same way. Brandy's family were Christians, and I sensed goodness in her too. Our Catholic family prayed the rosary and went to church now and then, but never missed church on Easter and Christmas. Mom's fascination with the occult sent mixed signals.

A large gold leather Bible sat as a statement piece in the middle of our living room coffee table. The colorful photographs and pages edged in gold drew me in. Evidence of its use through the years told me the contents offered something to treasure.

My dad had given it to my mother. I recall her telling me Dad often burglarized homes. That seemed strange to me. Why would my father take someone's family heirloom? Did he believe he could restore my mother's connection to God?

Sometimes I'd flip through the delicate pages when dusting the coffee table. One line that stood out said something about God commanding His angels to guard over us. Did He know the things going on in our home? How could a good God allow the violence and horror in our family? Why did I have to go through three fathers?

My hope in a good God bore no such evidence.

Not yet anyway.

Chapter 8

In celebration of Mom's divorce from Van, she threw a party. Her new job at The Elegant Inn, a fancy Greek restaurant, provided the perfect venue. The Pappas brothers owned the place, and they adored my mom. She often hung out there after her shift ended.

Mama didn't give me an allowance, and at age thirteen, there were things I wanted to do. Mom arranged my first job at the restaurant, bussing tables. She worked as a hostess during the week, and a cocktail waitress on weekends. In no time at all, Mom practically managed the bar.

The owners were happy to close the bar early for Mom's bash. With my stepfather finally gone, a celebration seemed appropriate. Mom invited anyone and everyone she knew. I even invited a couple of my friends.

Mom and I went shopping in her closet for something sexy to wear. My hormones were going crazy, right along with my thirty-one-year-old mother's. I picked out one of her silky polyester jumpsuits and held up the rust-colored, sleeveless, bell-bottomed outfit. It came with a matching silk belt tied around the waist. Holding the suit up against me, I asked with a big smile, "Can I wear this one?"

"I don't know. Try it on. See if it fits." She sifted through her dresser drawer. "Here, honey." She handed me a silk scarf.

"It's a little long." I lifted the pant legs from the shag carpet. "I'll have to wear my platforms." I took the scarf and tied it around my neck.

She kissed me on my head and whispered, "You look pretty, Scoochie."

The owners roped off the lounge to outside guests. When the dancing commenced, Mom said in a worried tone, "I'm going to go call Grandpa again. He should be here by now."

My grandfather owned a used-car lot a short distance from where Kelly's Bar used to be in downtown San Jose. My mom expected Grandpa to drive straight over after closing time. Mom called his house to see if he'd gone home to get his wife, but she hadn't heard from Grandpa either. Mom returned and ended the party abruptly.

Days later, Mom learned someone kidnapped Grandpa from his car lot while locking up the office for the night. I overheard Mom sobbing on the phone. "Dave, they found Daddy. ... They crushed his head. Oh, God! ... They found his body under a mattress at the docks in Oakland."

Tears welled at the news I just heard. "What? Mom! No! Not Grandpa!" My only protector. Now what?

We were in shock. The chatter about Grandpa's business with the mob convinced me his tendency to rip off the wrong people most likely led to his demise. Regardless, I knew our family secrets must not get out. That explained why nobody called for an investigation into his murder. Our family took things into their own hands and prepared to wage war against Grandpa's murderer. Dona called on a couple brothers she was friends with to help us out. They began hanging out at our house to offer some protection. The oldest brother,

Ron, looked much older than his eighteen years. His seductive way of flirting led to us having sex one night while my mother went out with a girlfriend after work. I knew I'd be in big trouble if my mother found out. Before Ron left my house that night, I asked him not to say anything about it.

I had to get away from the danger. The weight on my shoulders lifted when my mom granted permission for me to go away with my girlfriend, Melanie, and her mother for a weekend in Pismo Beach. My mom was close friends with Melanie's mom. I figured my mom wanted me to get away from the chaos. But upon returning from my weekend away, I walked in on Ron sleeping with my mom in her bed. I threw mom's shoes I had borrowed at her bedroom wall and stormed out of her room, seething. "I hate you both." I do not recall my mom trying to figure out the reason for my outburst. There were more serious things going on.

Mom mentioned to my uncle that she sensed someone followed her home from work. It didn't take long for Mom's words to become reality. A few nights later, she returned home shaken, describing an incident where someone had taken a shot at her while she was driving. The bullet hit the rear side panel of her car. My mom said it's a good thing I wasn't in the back seat, or I could've been dead.

The danger continued to intensify around our house. My uncles and step-grandmother were determined to retaliate against Grandpa's killer and remained armed with guns and knives at the funeral. My mom told me I did not have to walk up to Grandpa's casket. But this being my first funeral, my curiosity drew me to the front of the chapel of the mortuary.

I stood three feet away and caught a glimpse of Grandpa's head inside his casket. My neck tightened with a sense of fear. The extent of my grandfather's head wounds coupled with the heavy makeup made him unrecognizable. I hung my head with warm tears falling down my face.

The week following the funeral, Mom sat on watch, apprehensive about leaving for work. "See that car down the street?" Mom peeked between the long, dark living room curtains. She waved at me to hurry over to look out the window. "The dark-colored car parked up there at the corner. See it? They've been following me after work."

Leaning over the couch to get a look, I nodded.

She repeated with angst. "See it?"

"Yes, I see it!"

Two days later, I spotted the same car while walking to school in the morning. When it slowed. I picked up my pace. The car sped up. My pulse quickened. I took a side street to see if they would follow me. Mama, I'm scared. I whimpered inside. What if they shoot at me?

My rapid pulse pounded through my veins. Two men sat inside. I kept the car in my sights, careful not to make eye contact. I have to lose them. Caroline Davis Junior High School was several blocks away. My mind scattered, hoping to find a friend's house and get inside, and quick.

Darlene's house. I bolted through the gate into the side yard. I need to get home. No. That's not a safe place to be. I thought for sure one of them would jump out of the car and run after me. I pounded on the glass door with both hands. In seconds, Darlene rushed to the door. I let out a deep sigh. Oh, thank God.

"Hurry! Hurry!" Jumping up and down, I reached for the door handle right as my friend unlocked it.

She touched my shoulder. "You're scaring me. Are you okay?"

"Is your mom home?"

"Umm, no. She left for work already."

"Can you see if there's a dark car out front?"

Darlene looked out the kitchen window. "Coast is clear." She looked back at me. "What's going on?"

I sucked in a breath. "Some dangerous men are following me. It's a long story."

My friend's voice quivered. "Dangerous? Are they going to come back here looking for you?"

I reached for a tissue on the table. "I don't know. I need to call my mom. Can I use your phone, please?"

She widened her eyes. "Sure! Anything you need!" She handed me the push-button princess phone from the counter.

I dialed and clenched my fists, frustrated. "No answer."

Pointing to the living room window, I again asked Darlene if the dark car was gone. Her thumbs up assured me the car no longer lurked outside. I thanked my friend for her help and made my way home through the field instead of taking my normal route through the neighborhood. My heart skipped a beat at every crunch of leaves or scattering of rock along the path. What if the men are at our house? I don't even know if it's safe to go home.

After I told my mother about the men following me, she warned the family and sent for the troops. Grandpa Don's wife took all the kids living with her and went underground. My uncles built a brick fortress around their desert hideaway, equipped with cannons and a variety of automatic weapons.

We heard rumblings of Grandpa's possession of a small book the mob wanted. For whatever reason, we stayed put in our house on the hill. Not only did Aunt Dona's friends show up in force, but they brought their friends to protect us. Some were bikers, others were not.

More weapons, and even more drugs. I'm not sure how partying with loaded guns provided a safe place, but Mom considered it necessary to fend off the kidnappers.

One night, within an hour of returning from the Led Zeppelin concert at the Day on the Green in Oakland, the bikers launched into a huge fight in the front yard. I waited in suspense in the living room with two of my girlfriends who attended the concert with me. We watched while Ron attempted to break it up. He chased two guys off the property and threatened to shoot them.

Mom ran into the house, frantic. "Stay inside." Ron hurried past her.

Moments later, we heard what sounded like an explosion in our garage. The entire house shook. Ron loaded the shotgun and pushed past me at the front door. "Get back and stay inside."

I followed him outside. He pointed the loaded shotgun at the guy who had crashed through our garage door.

Mom's friends were supposed to keep trouble away, not bring more trouble. Ron dragged the guy out of the car and beat him with his bare hands, then chased him off at gunpoint. I wasn't sure why the neighbors never called the police. Afraid to get involved, I guessed.

After all the violence that night, I called my father. Jami had written letters to me nearly every week. I wanted to be with my sister again. This would be a great fresh start for me, especially since I'd be starting high school soon. Mom wasn't keen on the idea, though she understood my need to get out of harm's way. I packed up my things and left for Antioch on the Greyhound bus.

Jami introduced me to all her friends, who were usually my age. My cousins and father had a reputation that extended throughout the town. They assured me nobody would mess with me.

Going into ninth grade in Antioch translated to one more year in junior high. The upside to being a ninth-grader came with advantages similar to a senior in high school. My cousin, Mickey, told me the school principal knew our family name well. I knew the LaLanne's and Bennetts were a bunch of hellions and my father remained among them.

Dad continued dealing cocaine with his biker friends while running his appliance repair shop. I breathed easier, knowing he kept his club business quiet and mostly away from our house. I wished I'd known my father was dealing dope. He not only endangered himself, but also his wife, Jami, and me.

Rose, my new stepmother, was of Native American and Japanese descent and had thick, black hair down to her waist. She worked as a nurse in a convalescent home. Though soft-spoken, she kept my father in line.

Rose showed Jami and me the same love as her three natural-born children. They lived with their father, so I did not get to spend much time around them. Dad and Rose moved us from their tiny little one-bedroom rental into a bigger house. The corner lot gave us plenty of room. Jami and I shared the converted garage as our bedroom. We now lived only a few blocks away from our cousins and a few blocks from school.

In her letters, Jami described how often Dad grounded her. That didn't surprise me. My dad was much stricter than my mom. I don't know how I didn't get that.

One of his many rules included that we couldn't invite our friends over. He and Rose laid out rules to follow and chores to take care of. Dad expected dinner on the table when he got home from work at six o'clock. Homework must be done before leaving the house. Dad also forbade us from playing flag football until late at night at the park with our friends and cousins. The schedule felt suffocating, especially in comparison to my mother's futile attempt to enforce a 1:00 a.m. curfew. I missed the freedom to run.

Regardless, life appeared safer for me here, and Dad's rules gave me some sense that he cared. No fighting or drama allowed. Nobody messed with his girls. If they did, his biker brothers would set things straight.

When my dad's buddy, Jeff, offered to take me to see a movie at the drive-in, I thought nothing of it. Dad gave the green light. When Jeff got grabby with me, I warned him what my father would do to him if he touched me. He took me straight home and never said a word. This was my father's buddy. How could Dad not know his friend was a pig? I wondered if my father was okay with his friend messing around with his fourteen-year-old daughter. Then I remembered my dad cheating on my mother with our sixteen-year-old babysitter. She became his second wife. From then on, nobody could be trusted. Absolutely nobody.

I didn't belong here, either. At least, with Mom, I knew what to expect. Jami and I waited anxiously for our upcoming Christmas break. We both missed our mom and looked forward to our huge family gathering with my Aunt Marilyn, Grandma, my cousins, and the rest of our loud Sicilian family. I want my family back. I want my friends back. My freedom too. That, more than anything. When I talked to my mom, she made it sound like all the craziness had calmed down at her house. But then, she always held a twisted perception of what was safe and normal.

Christmas break gave me two weeks to catch up with my old friends and family. Christmas with my cousins gave me hope for some normalcy in our bloodline. I didn't want the time to end. Bobby missed me terribly. And I missed him.

With the bullying from our mother's immature boyfriend, my little brother had his own battle going on. I wanted to stay. More importantly, I needed to stay. Needed to protect my little brother from another monster.

And I'd learned the grass certainly was not greener on the other side. Our neighborhood. My friends. I knew I'd break Rose's heart. Dad's too.

Before they made the two-hour drive to pick us up that evening, I decided to stay with my mother. My heart hurt. Dad and Rose did their best to make a suitable home for me and Jami. I knew my father would be furious. And I wondered how Jami felt about Mom wanting her to move back home. Jami seemed happier living with Dad despite being grounded half the time.

Mom sat on the front porch, waiting for my father to pull up while Jami packed her things. "You better write me more letters." I sat on the edge of the bed, finding the words. "I'm sorry, Jami. I can't go back."

Her smile brought some calm to my nerves until Mom called us outside. My stomach churned. Trembling and barely able to speak, I walked toward my father. Rose sat in the passenger seat, smiling, waving at Mom.

Dad slid out of the car, happy to see us. We hugged, and I broke it to him. "Dad, I have something to tell you." I shifted my gaze from the ground to his eyes. "I want to stay here. I want to move back home with Mom."

My father stood for a second with a look of shock, processing what he heard. Enraged by my betrayal, he flipped me off while shouting foul words at me. My father and I became estranged from each other that night. Despite my heartbreaking pain, I also found it difficult to think about how easily he abandoned us a decade ago.

I still needed to forgive my father for many things.

But could I?

Chapter 9

Bitterness and unforgiveness toward both my father and step-father lingered, poisoning my every thought. To add insult to injury, Ron now lived with us after seducing me the night after my grandfather was murdered. The revelation that my mother chose to sweep more abuse under the rug enraged me. Every interaction with Ron was filled with the seething hatred I felt toward him.

Mom sold our house on the hill and rented a condominium a few miles away. Finally, she put an end to the madness and took charge of her life. I hoped this meant she truly desired a better life for her children. But Ron moved right along with us. The location provided easier access to places I could work, such as shopping centers and movie theaters. Plus, we lived close enough for me to walk to my new high school.

My friends, all self-proclaimed 'stoners', gathered before and after school at 'the rock', a giant boulder on the corner across the street from my school. While waiting for the morning bell one day, I started a conversation with Monica, an exceptionally striking girl from Uruguay with long, dark hair and European features. In new Dittos and platform shoes, topped with a modest blouse and gold jewelry, she stood out among the sea of jeans and leather jackets. When she told me she lived in the same condos, we bonded instantly. Monica knew everyone and where to find the parties. Over time, we talked about our complicated mom-daughter bonds and became even closer, like sisters.

Though we were always on the lookout for the next party, Monica and I also entered the workforce together. We landed summer jobs at Frontier Village, a western-themed amusement park, for their closing season. By the end of the summer, I saved enough money to cover the fees for driver's training. Passing my driving test meant I could finally borrow my mom's car, a gesture that spoke volumes about how proud she was. This taste of freedom helped me to keep working and away from home as much as possible.

Access to Mom's car also presented dangerous choices. By the age of sixteen, I easily passed for twenty-one, especially when I invaded my mother's closet for some of her more revealing clothes. Mom got a thrill showing me off as her 'sister' at the nightclubs she worked at.

I'll never forget my sixteenth birthday. Mom and I dressed up and hit every bar in town. Even being five years under the legal drinking age, the bouncers and bartenders, Mom's personal friends, gladly invited me in for a drink on the house. I was not carded one time throughout the night.

Returning to my mom's instilled a twisted sense of control. While I couldn't defy my father when I lived under his own roof, I held great disrespect for my mother. Our sisterly competition continued to diminish our mother-daughter relationship. Her wild ways set the tone for my own. Although I jumped back into the fire, navigating her chaotic world seemed doable. I remembered hearing a psychologist on a television show describe how some people thrive in chaos, because chaos is like a familiar friend. The words hit home for me.

I asked my Uncle Dave and Aunt Vicki if I could stay with them for a while. I looked up to my uncle. He and my aunt lived close enough to my school, so Mom gave me her blessing. Not that it mattered. After one week, my uncle climbed into bed with me when I was sound asleep. I couldn't believe it. Even he was not safe. I had no choice but to return to my mom's.

Despite the obstacles, I managed to adapt, but always felt like I was just barely hanging on. I began tattooing my body. A friend of a friend was a tattoo artist and gave me my first tattoo of a peacock on my left thigh. When the needle scraped my skin, the pain seemed to dull the ache in my soul, even though I couldn't quite understand why.

Painful blows continued in my life. Death seemed to follow my friends, taking them one by one for various reasons. I lost track of how many funerals I attended between the age of thirteen and sixteen. One friend, Dwayne, whom Jami dated during her visits to San Jose, took his own life. His mother found him in the garage, hanging from a bed sheet around his neck. His death rocked our entire high school. With most students planning to attend Dwayne's service, the school suspended classes for the day of the funeral. The crowd was so large that some friends stood in the hall, but that didn't stop everyone from belting out his anthem, "I'm as free as a bird now."

I had only ever encountered suicide in movies until it became a reality in my life. We were all left wondering what could have led Dwayne to commit suicide, and none of us had any answers. After crashing his stepfather's car while drinking, Dwayne admitted to his best friend that he was terrified of facing his parents. Though my life was bad, the thought of ending it all seemed extreme.

I wish someone could have done something. None of my friends knew what to say to each other. We were in a state of emotional shock, feeling nothing but confusion. People whispered about Dwayne spending eternity in hell. How could that be? My poor sister. Jami took it the hardest.

Alfred was the one who caused the deepest heartbreak I've ever known. In him, I found my first true love – an actual meaningful relationship with a boyfriend.

We often played Foreigner and Black Sabbath albums while getting high with our friends. I lost count of how many times he snuck me into the theater to watch The Song Remains the Same. Mom always mentioned his massive Cheshire cat grin.

Despite his frequent visits to juvenile hall, we all loved Alfred for his massive heart and sense of humor. One Friday night, Monica and I got ready to go to a party. The plan was to meet up with Alfred and his buddies at our usual party spot, Jack in the Box. When they did not show, we headed home. I waited all night with the phone near my pillow for Alfred's call.

The phone finally rang early the next morning. I about jumped out of my skin from anticipation. Instead, Monica's somber steady voice attempted to calm me. "Hon, Alfred passed away this morning. A junior from Santa Teresa High School stabbed him. Steve was with him." She paused, catching her breath in between sobs. "Something about stealing five dollars over beer. They operated for over eight hours. He didn't make it. I'm so sorry, Cherie."

In disbelief and shock, the tears took a minute. "Where was he? Who was he with?" Lying back on my bed, I tried to process the news. Monica could barely hold it together, yet I expected her to answer all my questions? My gut cramped. "Thank you for calling me right away." Grief stricken, I added, "I gotta go. Please…please let me know if you hear anything more." I clenched my head with my hands.

Jolted awake by the sound of my gasps and sobs, my mom peeked into my room. Seeing me curled up on my bed, she hurried to my side. She gently brushed my hair from my face., "Honey, are you okay? What happened?" My mother's eyes welled when her eyes met my red and swollen ones.

I couldn't speak. She wrapped me in a hug, doing everything she could to comfort and calm me.

Wailing uncontrollably in the unexpected solace of her embrace, I emptied myself in a hurricane of grief. "Mom, I loved him so much. Why him? Oh, God. Why?"

Mom stood by my side through it all, including his funeral. The weight of her support through my grief transcended the prior harbored grievances and insurmountable disagreements. We shared the burdens of our sorrows together in a sacred communion of shared pain, first through the loss of her father and now my first love. My mother transformed into an unyielding rock of comfort, revealing the profound depth of her love for me.

The students of Oak Grove High School honored Alfred's memory by shutting down classes, just like they had for Dwayne. I couldn't wait to see Alfred. His profile was only partially visible from inside the open casket, making it difficult for me to gather the courage to approach. Like a grieving widow, I wanted to kiss him goodbye. But what would people think?

Sitting in the front row, I watched family and friends express their memories. Mom squeezed my hand through every tear. My stomach in knots, I walked up just as the others returned to their seats. I wasn't sure what came over me, but I held his hand and kissed his forehead. Despite the coolness of his skin, his smile warmed my heart. His parents were so sweet to me that day, even in their unimaginable grief.

In honor of Alfred, Monica and I planned an enormous party. We posted flyers up and down Blossom Hill Road around the mall. My plans got flipped when I jumped on the back of some guy's Harley at a red light. We went off on a run along Highway 1 with the club Scott rode with. I passed a bottle of Peppermint Schnapps back and forth with one of the other girls on the bike next to us. I guess I blacked out at some point because Scott secured me to the back of the bike with his belt to get me home.

I woke up on the couch to the soft warmth of the sun on my face streaming in through the living room window. Groggy, with my head throbbing, panic struck. "Oh, no. What time is it? I'm going to be late for my own party!"

The party had gone on without me. I called Scott, and he picked me up to join him at his sister's birthday party. All I wanted was for him to take me as his ol' lady. The bad news was the others at the party made it clear I was much too young for Scott. I couldn't understand why I wasn't wearing a property patch by now.

I supposed it took this incident to shake me up a bit. Alcoholism ran rampant in my bloodline. I knew better. Right when I was starting to feel at home in my high school, my mom broke the news that we were moving to a new place in a different school district.

The only friend I made there betrayed me. I began cutting school right away. My teacher called a meeting with my mom and me. To save my GPA, she recommended I skip my senior year and take the California High School Proficiency Exam. Mrs. Morgan peeked above her thin, metal-rimmed glasses at me. "You could start making a salary of around forty thousand a year with your math skills, young lady."

I took her advice and graduated in my junior year. I still had no idea how I could move out while earning minimum wage. Fortunately, I found a job working at The Sizzler where I earned cash tips.

One night, after working the closing shift, I felt exhausted and drained. Taking the bus from downtown San Jose all the way out to our new apartment on the south side of town took an additional hour.

I mustered the last bit of energy I had to open our front door. Frantically fumbling or my keys, I remained aware of movement in my peripheral vision. With my hands trembling, I fumbled with the key before finally getting it into the lock and pushing open the warped wooden door with my other hand, trying not to drop the food from work. I hated working the closing shift and the night wasn't going well since I had done most of the cleaning. The need to constantly watch over my shoulder only fueled my anger. I've got to get out of this place. I'm going to die here.

Days before, the ex-girlfriend of Mom's new biker boyfriend, Manuel, came looking for my mother. Caroline's fists pounding hard on the door sounded like it might be another visit from the feds. Fortunately, I'd remembered to put the chain across the door when I came home from work only minutes earlier. When I opened the door, Caroline had a massive knife and was trying to reach at me through the small crack in the door. Slurring her words, she yelled, "Let me in! Get your mother!"

My heart raced, and I jumped back to avoid her slicing my face. I grabbed her wrist. With all my strength, I pushed against the door and let go of her arm. The heavy knife fell against my ankle when the door slammed shut. I didn't feel the blade slice across my ankle amidst the commotion until I saw the blood.

My mother wanted to kill Caroline. Come to find out, when Manuel got together with Mom, he still lived with her. One of Manuel's buddies told me Caroline called him, crying for help after Manuel handcuffed her by her ankles to their coffee table to keep her from following him. Once freed from her shackles, Caroline got even by burying all his guns and knives in the backyard. Then, she came after Mom.

Knowing what Manuel did to this woman left me wondering how my mother could allow him in our life. Manuel, standing at six foot four, had calloused and tar-stained hands larger than those of an average man. He wore size fourteen leather boots. His brown leather midnight rider hat sat low on his head, framing his shoulder-length black hair.

Mom talked proudly of Manuel's Portuguese heritage. I remembered how she spoke of Little Joe with the same respect. Manuel collected every type of weapon, not just guns and knives. Mom told me his brother served twenty-five years in prison for blowing up his ol' lady's car. Manuel and his cousins associated with the Hells Angels, and they often went target shooting or hunted wild boar. Manuel didn't care much for my brother and me hanging around the apartment. He bullied Bobby often and controlled whom I invited over.

I switched jobs for a salesclerk position at a new retail store within walking distance of our apartment. My manager scheduled me for as many shifts I could take. I pocketed gold trinkets while unpacking shipments of jewelry. The tension of stealing gave me a rush. Working the closing shift also gave me the chance to adjust the inventory numbers without anyone else around. I wondered if stealing helped me gain some form of control in my life. The circumstances at home continued to escalate between my mom and Caroline with her showing up unexpectedly and calling all hours of the night. My mom wanted her dead.

Little did I know what was in store for me one night after work. Stepping into our townhouse, I immediately noticed the illumination coming from the light at the top of the stairway on the left side of the room. My mother yelled from the top of the stairs, "Stop right there!" She clutched her .38, aimed right at me.

I gasped, hoping my announcement wasn't a split second too late. "Mom, it's me!" I covered my face with my hands. This is it. It's finally my time. Trembling, I waited for her to pull the trigger. The image of my Aunt Belle firing bullets into the side of our van on Christmas Eve was etched into my mind. I could almost hear the sound of the shots ringing in my ears.

I can't remember how I moved from Mom's line of fire. The rest of that night is one big blur.

All that mattered now was leaving home for good. I couldn't handle any more. But hopelessness consumed me when I could not find a way out of my circumstances. Anxiety and fear took hold again. I briefly entertained suicidal thoughts. I knew I needed to remove myself from the situation as quickly as possible.

A month later, Monica and I met a couple guys at a Day on the Green concert at the Oakland Coliseum. Flaunting our summer bodies, we danced at the front of the green to the music of REO Speedwagon, Kansas, and .38 Special.

I leaned close to my friend's ear while we squeezed through the marijuana-hazed crowd, "I think this is as close as we're going to get without getting crushed." We were rocking out to the music when I spotted a couple of cute guys sitting in the backstage bleachers. The one with the great smile waved. I nudged Monica's arm. "Hey, see that guy up there?" I pointed, trying to get her eyes to align with the distant speck at the end of my finger. "Do you see him?"

We both waved. Eye contact!

I used some flirty sign language to arrange a meeting spot at the gated entrance to the backstage bleachers. He flashed us a big smile from the other side of the cyclone fencing. Todd and his friend lived in Sacramento, about two hours from San Jose. He gave me his phone number, and for the first time, I felt like there was a way out.

REO Speedwagon serenaded me with the cool ocean breeze from the San Francisco Bay blowing through my hair. Standing against the rail on the second level of the Oakland Coliseum Stadium, I closed my eyes. And smiled.

There's nothing holding me here. It's time for me to fly.

Chapter 10

Todd and I dated for three months before he asked me to live with him. I called Mom with the news. A contentious discussion followed with me mentioning I was following in her footsteps by leaving at an early age—seventeen. She couldn't argue but ripped me with some choice words. Words her own mother spewed, more than likely.

Two months later, she begged me to come visit her. For some reason, I agreed. Setting out on the drive from Sacramento to San Jose, the green rolling hills of Sunol rushed by and I felt a sense of freedom wash over me. I didn't have to go home, but I wanted Mom to know I still loved her. And I had to check on my little brother.

My grip on the steering wheel tightened involuntarily as I made the steep climb over Mission Summit. Tears welled up at the first sight of the Santa Clara Valley floor. The heaviness in my chest made it difficult to breathe. In the midst of traffic, I grappled with the intensity of emotions, desperately trying to navigate both the physical and emotional turmoil while inching closer to a reunion I dreaded. What am I doing? Why am I going back? I hate this place. Wiping the tears from my eyes, I caught my breath. It's only for a couple of days. It's okay, Cherie. There's nothing to be afraid of.

Thick grayish-brown smog blanketed the buildings in the distance. The setting sun appeared as a dark orange fireball, suffocated with the haze of the polluted air. The darkness disturbed my spirit. Trying my best to shake it off, I made the turn into the neighborhood of dingy brown townhomes.

The street, lined with banged up automobiles, reminded me of the wreckage left behind. The sight of Bobby on a skateboard brought on a sudden rush of guilt for leaving him in that place. A lump formed in my throat. It's not like I could have taken him with me. I honked my horn to get his attention.

Dropping his board, my little brother ran toward me. "Sissy!"

Bobby's blond hair and blue eyes, inherited from both our mother and his father, set him apart from Jami and me.

The next morning, Bobby, who just celebrated his ninth birthday, asked me if I would blow dry his hair like I used to. He loved it when I helped him get ready for school. Except for the morning I poured brown soap on his pancakes. Grandma Mary had repurposed an old Aunt Jemima syrup bottle, filling it with a dark detergent. Mom mistakenly placed it in our pantry. Bobby never missed a chance to tease me about that incident.

I missed those mornings with my brother. I recognized Bobby's need for me to be there with him when I saw Manuel subjecting him to bullying. A fierce anger ignited within me. Manuel's buddies were no different and taunted Bobby at every turn. Determined not to let this situation consume me any longer, I pushed my thoughts aside. The looming responsibility of finding employment awaited me back home, accompanied by a nagging guilt that threatened to unsettle my heart. However, bringing Bobby along was not an option. I reassured him with a promise to visit again soon.

The next day, I woke with my brother on my mind. I had to shake off the guilt and focus on a positive mindset. He's not your responsibility, Cherie. Now, you've got this.

Shifting my thoughts helped me ace my job interview. I'd always breezed through interviews, but this one was a big deal. The moment I secured the full-time bookkeeper position for the wholesale security systems distributor, my career in accounting took off. As soon as Cindy, our new receptionist, began working, I knew we were gonna be best friends and partners in crime.

Between my salary and Todd's wages working as a machinist, we could move into our own little place right away. Todd turned twenty-one shortly after that. Through him, I discovered a new world beyond the confines of my sheltered upbringing.

Todd was one of six children, him being the second youngest. His family reminded me of the classic *Leave it to Beaver* family. Wholesome is the best way to describe them. Todd's parents successfully raised all their kids together while maintaining a strong, lasting marriage.

My father, in comparison, had experienced three marriages and fathered a total of seven children from those relationships, three of which were stepchildren. My Grandpa Don had wives and kids all over the place.

Todd's parents retired from stable careers. Their kids went to college. Knowing a normal family that goes on vacation and stays together gave me hope for the same.

Todd suggested an impromptu adventure after we settled into our duplex. The drive into the Sierra Nevada Mountains took my breath away. Approximately an hour into our journey, a magical transformation occurred—the ground turned into a dazzling expanse of white.

Excitement surged through me, causing my eyes to widen, and I couldn't help but exclaim, "Oh my gosh. It's snow."

Todd laughed and turned up the heat in the truck. "Well, you're in for a treat, my dear. You're about to see a whole bunch of it here real soon." Pulling off the highway, we drove down the long snow-covered road to the parking lot at Boreal Mountain Resort.

With a childlike wonder, I asked, "What is this?"

Unbuckling his seat belt, he flashed a big smile my way. "We're going skiing!"

His enthusiasm told me I was in for a treat. Todd and his older brother, Ray, were expert skiers. They worked seasonal jobs as Ski Patrol at Sugar Pine Ski Resort.

Todd paid for our tickets, and we headed to the ski shop where he bought me a jumpsuit. Next, we walked to the rental area to fit me for skis, boots, and poles. I couldn't believe this. I looked at my boyfriend. "Man, I'm lucky." I'd never imagined doing things like skiing.

He spent close to an hour trying to teach me how to snowplow without crashing into a tree. I knew I was pushing his buttons when I saw him take a deep breath and exhale slowly. I encouraged him to hit the Black Diamond run while I kept practicing on the bunny hill.

Watching five-year-old children in ski school gave me a jolt of confidence. If they can do this with no poles, I can do it! After several trips on the ski lift, I mastered the bunny hill. Frequent weekend ski trips with Todd increased my confidence on the ski runs. Before I knew it, I was cruising the intermediate runs. Flying down the mountain, I felt alive and untouchable, free from all my past worries.

The constant chaos I once knew no longer consumed me. I tried to visit my family every couple of weeks. I missed them dearly, but my mood shifted every time I reached the last twenty-minute stretch of the drive. I also found out Van had returned to San Jose to spend time with Bobby. The thought of seeing Van kept my visits few and far between.

Maintaining boundaries with my family impacted how often I saw the friends I'd left behind. I missed Monica most of all, but she moved to Washington state, got married, and had a baby immediately after high school. When she moved back to California a few years later, we picked up right where we left off. But something was different about her. Monica's countenance exuded so much more than mere maturity. Peace.

I assumed the reason for her newfound joy might be because of her time away from San Jose. Our conversation led her to tell me she accepted Jesus Christ as her Lord and Savior. Curious, I asked, "So, you're a Christian now? Is that what you mean?" I recalled the weight of the conversation back in high school when Monica confided about her traumatic past. She painfully recalled the details of the time her mother attempted to kill her when she was young. Monica lived with constant torment, questioning if her mother had ever truly loved her, while enduring tremendous pain and trauma for many years. Now it all seemed to be in the past.

During one of our phone calls, she invited me to attend a Christian women's retreat at her new church. I tried to get the words out, but they stuck in my throat. For a split second, my thoughts flashed to the televangelist scandals I'd seen on television. Though I did recognize a genuine change in Monica, I wasn't up for the three-day adventure. Delicately, I said, "Uh…I appreciate you thinking of me, but I'm going to pass this time."

My precious friend did not give up on me. The next time I saw her, she was in Sacramento for her daughter's beauty pageant. We met for lunch at a trendy restaurant on the Sacramento River. After catching up with the things most best friends talk about. Monica reached into her large leather tote and pulled out a paperback novel. She laid the book, worn and earmarked throughout, in front of me on the round bistro table. Her hand resting on the faded cover, Monica looked intently into my eyes. "Here, I think you should read this book. I know how much you love to read."

The front cover contained an image of a church in the center of a foreboding storm, with angel wings ominously hovering above. This Present Darkness, printed in large fiery lettering, intrigued me.

I read the back cover. "Hmmm, sounds scary. Frank Peretti, huh? I love thrillers. Is this like Stephen King's books?"

Monica said Peretti was a Christian author of fiction. "I got to hear Frank Peretti speak at my church. He wrote the story to explain what goes on around us in the spiritual realm. Keep it."

I placed the book in my bag and thanked her. I didn't have the guts to tell Monica she sounded like a Jesus freak. Nevertheless, her newly discovered faith changed the trajectory of her life. In that moment, I pondered the shift occurring in both our lives.

In the upcoming weeks, my heart stirred with anticipation, nudging me to read Peretti's novel. The way he wrote about the spiritual realm of good against evil resonated in my mind. Memories of messing around with the Quija board and my mother's fascination with psychics and astrology raised many questions. I wondered how God could allow so much evil to surround our family. Without a doubt, I lived most of my life in darkness.

The following weekend, I packed the book to take with me on our camping trip to Ice House Reservoir. We expected it would take close to an hour and a half to get there. Todd did not believe in normal camping. He only camped in the wilderness. No campsites or bath-rooms. In our excitement, we neglected to consider Friday afternoon traffic. Navigating the forest after dark made it impossible to set up camp. Todd parked my new Toyota 4x4 just off the highway in a clearing covered in pine needles. We decided to sleep in the camper with his hunting dog, Drake, and look for a spot at sunrise.

Chilled air woke me. "It's freezing!" I sat up to look out the window. "Uh-oh, we've got snow." My excitement deflated. "So much for camping."

Todd rubbed my shoulder with reassurance. "It's okay. We can still take a drive up to Loon Lake."

I did not give it a second thought. Afterall, my new mud and snow tires were made for trips like this. Besides, I trusted Todd. He knew the area and practically lived outdoors. I imagined the gorgeous, crisp blue water nestled among the ponderosa pines in the Sierra Nevada Mountains. We were west of Lake Tahoe, and the drive would take us to an elevation of 6,500 feet.

Fresh fallen snow draped the forest. Our truck hugged the hillside, climbing farther up the mountain. I peered out my window down Ice House Canyon in wonder. Breathtaking! I'd never been anywhere like this, having grown up in Silicon Valley, California. Heading for the beach over Highway 17 through the Santa Cruz Mountains was about it for me.

The canyon floor grew more distant at every turn. Half way up the winding canyon, the tires hit ice beneath the snow, spinning in our attempt to climb Ice House Road. I instinctively gripped the passenger handle above my head. Todd stopped to lock in the four-wheel-drive. But that only made a slight difference. A few minutes later, Todd said, "I think we better turn around. It doesn't look like these tires will take us up to the lake after all. We'll do Loon Lake another time"."

Quick to agree, I asked, "How are you going to turn around here? The road is way too narrow."

He slowly maneuvered the truck. I couldn't watch. Trying not to hold my breath, I grabbed the handle tighter and felt my feet trying to push through the floorboard.

In a calm, steady tone, Todd reminded me, "I've driven this road many times. We're fine. Trust me." He pulled out from the three-point turn. "You can open your eyes now. We'll take our time and head home."

The downshift of the gears slowed us to a crawl while descending the mountain. I didn't think we could have gone any slower. I eased my grip from the handle to make the drive less stressful for Todd. I tried to laugh while fighting against the fear. "At least the hillside is on my side of the road this time."

My eyes doubled in size when the truck slid a couple of feet. I gasped, tightening my grip.

Todd's eyes remained fixed on the road. Still calm, he said, "Just a little black ice. It's okay." The road curved to the right. But the truck continued to slide forward. Todd remained calm, yet prepared. "Hold on. We're going for a ride."

We headed straight for the canyon. When the truck met the edge of the icy road, my heart sunk. I imagined us flying over the cliff. Both hands pressed against the liner above me, bracing for impact. I screamed, "God, please! No!"

With the front of the truck dipped over the edge of the mountain, the bottom of the three-mile canyon wall stared right at me. Everything seemed to move in slow motion. My ears closed up. The truck came to a stop. Barely able to breathe and still bracing myself, I couldn't see anything that would have stopped us from lunging down the canyon. Maybe an army of angels?

Todd surveyed the parameter of the truck from his limited view in the driver's seat. He said something, but I could not make out his words. Our small Toyota pickup teetered over the edge of the mountain. "Get out of the truck," Todd said calmly. "Slowly." He pulled the emergency brake with his foot standing on the brake pedal. "Honey, I need you to get out of the truck. Don't make any quick movements. Gather rocks and branches and wedge them in front of the back tires."

I took a deep breath, opened my door, and cautiously stepped down from the truck. I followed his instructions, hopeful to keep the truck from rolling into the canyon. I managed to pull Drake out of the camper, removing eighty pounds from the front of the truck. I tried leveling the ground behind the tires with our camp shovel. The cold air and high altitude shortened my breathing. Todd tested the leverage. I gasped when the truck slipped forward. Frantic, I dug my hands into the snow, lifting boulders onto the tailgate of the truck. Our plan to balance the truck's weight failed as the rocks shifted towards the front. By now, throbbing pain settled into my shoulders. Keep going. Keep moving, Cherie. Resist the cold. I fought the urge to let the tears flow, holding them back with all my strength. I couldn't see a way to help. My hands burned. I could barely move my fingers. I begged Todd to jump.

Firmly but calmly, he said, "Okay, I need you to back away from the truck." He assessed the slope and terrain of the mountain and pointed down the canyon wall. "I see a spot about three hundred feet down with manzanita brush and some boulders. I'm gonna kamikaze this thing into it."

I stepped back and hugged Drake around his neck. "God, please help him. Please!"

With the quick release of the emergency brake, Todd maneuvered the truck toward his target. The truck stopped precisely where he described. I warmed my frozen hands with my breath, waiting for a sign of life from below. Todd stepped from the wreckage, yelling and jumping up and down, waving his arms around. He took a few minutes to collect himself, then hiked up the steep canyon wall with our sleeping bags and other necessities.

I cried with gratitude. "You did it! You're okay!" I yelled. "Thank you, God!"

We held each other, crying tears of relief and pain. Drake leaned into our legs. A subtle change in the atmosphere caught Todd's attention. He took Drake back down to the truck, locked him in the camper, and returned with more gear.

Slushy ice pelted us from the sky. The force of the wind grew stronger by the second. Todd secured his sleeping bag around his body with a belt. "I need to get to the ranger station and find some help. You'll need to wrap up." He pointed to a ledge in the hillside. "Here's a spot where you'll be protected from the wind and ice." I stood by his every word, in wonder of his natural survival instincts.

Tucked in the rocky hillside ledge, my eyes remained locked on him until his image disappeared around the bend. I recalled Todd mentioning the ranger station and U.S. Forest Service were closed for the season. We were the only crazies up here. Fearful thoughts attacked my mind, and I shook uncontrollably. What if he can't continue? What if he's hurt? Nobody is going to find us! My legs cramped and my feet hurt terribly. God, if that was you, please help us.

The storm continued raging through the canyon. I blew warm breath into my hands, clenching the sleeping bag. I struggled with the fear of falling asleep and not waking.

Hours passed. We'd headed out at daybreak.

I woke to the hum of a truck engine. Todd walked toward me, wrapped in a large blanket. I glanced at my watch, wiping the moisture from its face. Ten o'clock. Wow. The entire morning felt like a dream. He helped me out of the rocky crevice. An elderly man and his wife sat inside the cab of an old Ford pickup truck with a young boy seated between them.

Todd explained he'd made it several miles toward the highway when he spotted the truck coming toward him. The couple were out for an early Saturday morning drive with their grandson. He couldn't have been more than five years old. They pulled over when they saw Todd covered in snow.

The men assessed the scene of the accident. Todd made one last hike down the snow-covered mountain to retrieve Drake from the camper. Before long, we were off the mountain at the ranger station. Todd thanked the nice couple and assured them we could call our family from the pay phone. Someone would come get us.

After an hour of trying to reach family early on a Saturday morning, Todd spotted the truck again. "Hey, they're coming back!"

The sweet woman stepped down from the cab carrying hot chocolate and pastries. "We thought you could use something to warm you up. You must be hungry." Their grandson watched through the window of the cab of the truck. They man asked where we were from and offered to take us wherever we needed to go.

Todd warmed his hands around the cup of hot cocoa. "Sacramento," Todd said, shivering.

The woman smiled sweetly at her husband. "That's where we're from. What part of Sacramento?"

"Fair Oaks, near Madison Avenue," I said.

Their eyes brightened and the man laughed. "Well, I'll be. We live on Enfield Street, right near there." He motioned to the truck. "Get in."

I could not believe my ears. Could this be for real? But then, I had read in Peretti's book about angels protecting people. I also remember reading about that in my mother's giant Bible. We loaded up in the truck and in amazement. I said to Todd, "If you didn't believe in God before, I bet you do now."

Stunned with awe and wonder, we stepped out from the backseat of the cab of their truck onto the driveway of our duplex. The woman motioned toward the end of the street. "Yep, we live just down at the end of Enfield. Don't be strangers now, okay?" Her smile warmed my heart. We hugged them and thanked them for everything.

God felt real in that moment. It never occurred to me angels could appear as a grandmother and grandfather. Sharing the Ice House miracle with family and friends brought further clarity about that day. Todd's brother-in-law happened to work for Cal Trans. When Todd described the accident over the phone, his brother-in-law was all too familiar with the area. He arranged for a large tow truck to recover my truck that night. He told Todd he'd only recovered dead bodies from that canyon and declared us a living miracle. No signs of damage were visible on my truck when the tow truck pulled it from the canyon. Todd drove it home the very same night. People couldn't believe our story. No damage. No injuries or broken bones.

Would God call on His angels to rescue us?

But why?

Chapter 11

Despite our miracle, when Todd left for his fishing and hunting weekends, I went out drinking with girlfriends. This made me an easy target for men. Our wedding date grew closer, while my feet grew colder. One night, I confided in Monica about cheating on Todd.

She told me, "Cherie, you need to make up your mind. Todd is a good man, and he loves you."

I knew that. But, even so, when the day came, I choked on my wedding vows while forcing down my tears. One week away from my twenty-first birthday, standing in paradise, and I could not fathom a lifelong commitment to someone as good as Todd. The glass of champagne I chugged sent my head spinning as the sun set over Waimea Falls Park. Getting married in Hawaii was a girl's dream, but it all felt like a big lie.

Am I really doing this? For the rest of my life? Yes, I need to do this.

Why am I so afraid?

Straighten up, Cherie. He's a good man. There's no way I'll ever find another like him.

Maybe he is good for me. To protect me from myself.

My wedding day was not exactly what I'd dreamed of. My father didn't want to fly to O'ahu, even when I offered to cover his airfare and hotel costs. He gave me some lame excuse that he'd already seen Hawaii. Our small group of eight, including Todd's parents, my mom, the best man, my matron of honor, and another one of Todd's buddies made the day intimate.

Until I spotted a man in the distance, walking across the grounds of Waimea Falls Park right toward us. Squinting through my intoxicated vision, his black cowboy hat and jeans came into focus. In disbelief, I asked, "Is that Manuel? What the hell is he doing here? He wasn't invited." I turned to my mom for answers.

My mother squealed. "He wanted to be with me. How sweet."

I could either ruin our wedding day or make the best of it, so I kept my cool. At our reception dinner at the top of the Hyatt in Waikiki, Manuel graciously insisted on covering our tab. Afterward, Todd and I walked the strip through Waikiki, he in his white tuxedo, and me in my lacey princess bridal gown. The howls and whistles from the surrounding tourists and locals topped off our evening.

Weeks before our wedding, Jami, her boyfriend Tommy, and their newborn baby boy, Robert, had moved in with us. She wanted a better life for her son, and we were there to help them get a fresh start. While traveling home from our honeymoon, we received word that our landlord sent them packing.

Apparently, they held a big party at our house, and broke into the neighbor's van to steal a keg of beer. That ended their fresh start. Jami ended up moving back to San Jose.

Mom helped Jami out by letting her move into the townhouse she rented, while Mom moved in with Manuel. I wasn't sure how it happened, but Van also stayed with Bobby, Jami, Tommy, and their son, Little Robert, in the townhouse. I felt awful for my poor sister. She was a wreck with Van around. Jami and Tommy fought horribly.

Despite marrying someone safe and good, the urge to run from Todd continued. I could not comprehend why I would return to my dysfunctional, violent, lawless world. At times, I thought this good life appeared too good to be true. And I would do all I could to destroy it before anyone else could.

On one visit to San Jose, I sought out an old boyfriend. This led to a three-month affair. When Todd asked me for a divorce through his tear-filled eyes, I woke up to the severity of my infidelity.

"I don't know. I'm sorry. I love you. I think I need to see a counselor." My guilt-ridden sorrow ran deep as I reflected on the numerous times I'd cheated on Todd leading up to our wedding day. Discussing the possibility of divorce shook sense into me. I could not understand why I was prone to self-sabotage. I don't even think I fully realized what that was. Not only did I jeopardize my marriage but my work suffered, equally. My manager restructured my job duties. The tension was palpable. She knew I had been skimming cash from the per diem envelopes. My work reflected the weight of my personal issues. I resigned before she could fire me.

Todd's boundary gave me the determination to remain a faithful wife for the duration of our marriage. Even more so, to break the generational cycle of divorce in my family. Seeing a counselor, though invasive, proved to be the best decision for us. Todd forgave me and agreed to move forward.

Within a couple weeks of leaving my last job, I secured a position as Accounting Manager with a credit union, I knew this was my shot at a great career. Determined to demonstrate my competence, I audited their processes and established an impressive framework of internal controls. When I made it difficult for others to commit fraud or embezzle, I didn't feel as tempted myself. My goal was to prove to myself that I could achieve a normal existence.

The CEO acknowledged my performance and promoted me within my first year. My wardrobe budget increased to look the part and fit in with the rest of the professionals. Working weekends and evening became my norm. When not working, Todd and I spent time with my friends from work and their spouses.

Meanwhile, Todd and his older brother, Mark, went into business and opened a machine shop. When Mark put our business investment and assets in jeopardy, tempers flared at the shop. The fact that Todd would not confront his brother infuriated me.

Night terrors frequented my sleep. They became increasingly violent, with me acting out homicidal tendencies. One night I dreamed I trapped my brother-in-law in his house and set it on fire. I woke up startled yet validated. Oh my gosh, that felt so real! My body trembling uncontrollably, I cried into my pillow. Why do I have so much hate for him? Yes, I wanted to kill him to end the threat against our well-being. But I clearly had a much bigger problem. Homicidal thoughts tormented me every time I saw him or thought of him, and I couldn't tell my husband. Or anyone.

Drinking resulted in deeper depression. Over time, the episodes increased in frequency. Hostility and heaviness shifted toward me in the darkness of my bedroom, enshrouding me in sadness and despair. I couldn't take the perpetual sense of rage, fear, and shame pressing me into this pit of hopelessness and despair anymore.

I contemplated how I would end my life. I'm tired of trying so hard to fit in. Nobody knows the real Cherie. They can't know me. I can't hide any longer. Deep down, I questioned if demons were trying to take me down. How could I be such a mess when I had everything I ever dreamed of? As hard as it was to admit, I needed professional help.

While at the office one Saturday morning, I browsed the yellow pages for a counselor. The young woman who took my call at a women's crisis center referred me to a local support group for survivors of trauma and abuse.

Running late after work to my first session, I approached the small modular building. The location could not be more difficult to find. Frustrated, I opened the door and scoped out the room, dull with gray walls and flooring. My shoulders tightened, and a knot formed in my stomach. Skipping lunch did not help. About a dozen middle-aged men and women formed a circle in the middle of the room. I took a seat among them. How in the world did I end up with a co-ed group? I excused myself and walked out.

Shortly after that experience, my doctor prescribed Prozac. I'd heard positive things about this antidepressant from a couple of my coworkers. At this point, I'd try anything.

To my surprise, the depth of my depression worsened. The idea of relying on these drugs for the rest of my life scared me. Why did I still want to kill myself? Most days, I could barely get out of bed.

In the dead of night, I was jolted awake by the sensation of something thumping against my feet. I kicked the sheets. Still … thumping. Holding my breath, I tried not to move. I looked over at my husband, who was sound asleep. Pulling up the covers did not make the thumping stop.

Convinced that little demons were jumping on my feet, I jerked my legs. Curled in a fetal position, I clenched my hands and hid my face in my pillow. Oh, God, make them go away. My body trembling,

I squeezed my eyes closed. I couldn't wake up my husband. He'd think I'd lost my mind.

Immersing myself in work occupied my mind. The credit union CEO requested I move my office into her private work annex which was followed by another promotion to Financial Analyst. Traveling for work overshadowed my personal woes. Our social circle grew as a result of company events. I strived for more toys, more clothes, jewelry, and a higher salary. I wanted it all and stepped on as many toes as necessary to land the next opportunity. Having a beautiful home, toys, a great career, and a faithful husband never seemed enough. Todd recognized how important my career was. After selling the machine shop, he fell into an emotional slump. I became the breadwinner.

When his brother-in-law showed up at our new house on his Harley Davidson, I suggested we buy one too. Todd loved to ride, anyway. How exhilarating to be on a bike again! I enjoyed riding on the back, as always. But I couldn't deny the stirring in me to learn how to ride solo. Todd laughed at the idea. When his brother-in-law mentioned his plans to ride up to the Northern California redwoods for the infamous Redwood Run, we jumped at the opportunity. This would be my first time joining a rally with thousands of bikers.

We packed up the bike with clothes and rain gear. The kitchen vibrated when Todd fired up the bike in the garage.

I peeked my head out the door, waving to get his attention. "Hey, we need to stop at the credit union. I forgot to get cash."

He nodded and backed the bike down the driveway.

The office was the last place I wanted to be this weekend. I'd make it quick so management would not recognize me. Dressed in full leathers, I entered the lobby of the building. Seeing one of my friends behind the teller window brought a wave of relief over me. I pulled off my helmet.

Teresa needed a second before she squealed, "Cherie, is that you?" Her smile revealed her surprise.

I felt the blood rush to my cheeks. I laughed to shake off the awkwardness. "Yep, it's me. I guess I look a little different, huh?"

My friend leaned through the teller window to admire my leather chaps. "Wow, girl! You need to hang out with JoAnn. She has her own motorcycle." Her enthusiasm made me nervous.

I kept my voice low and wrapped up my business. I don't know what I expected when I appeared in my riding gear, but it wasn't that. Revealing this side of who I was might cause my boss to think less of me. Some things were best to remain unknown.

Back on the bikes, we made one more stop at Granzella's, a popular Italian place, to meet up with Todd's cousin, Dave, who would ride up with us. Dave was a big, burly, red-bearded biker. He hung his helmet on his handlebar and ran across the street, dodging cars as we pulled into the parking lot. The guys did their brotherly bonding, and we were off. The family camaraderie set the tone for the rest of the weekend.

Riding with a group of bikes again energized my soul. I felt significant, part of something powerful and rebellious. Dave was a true biker. Not like Todd and his brother-in-law. They loved motorcycles, but riding ran through Dave's blood. A biker knows a true biker versus a poser. I didn't feel like such an outcast with him riding with us.

Packs of bikes roared through the rolling hills blanketed with blue lakes and green vineyards. Every version of motorcycle—choppers, full dressers, rat bikes, show bikes, and even one decorated like a buffalo—caused a backup and traffic came to a sudden stop on U.S.

101 through Main Street in Willits. The small Northern California town displayed a grand arch that straddled the highway, marking the Gateway to the redwoods, and paid homage to the railroad and Willits Frontier Days. The Run to the Redwoods drew people from all over the country. The roar of our bikes sounded like thousands of wild horses.

Most packed enough gear to stay for a week or longer with their tents, duffel bags, sleeping bags, and saddle bags carrying everything from tools to rain gear. Dave signaled for us to park the bikes outside an old warehouse dedicated to the collection and preservation of antique logging and railroad equipment.

With a rumbling stomach and a desire to watch people, I leaned on Todd's shoulder, raising my voice so he could hear me through his helmet. "I saw an open table on the patio at the 101 Drive-In. I'll run and grab it for us." It took me a minute to stretch my legs and pull off my helmet and gloves. I gave Todd a quick kiss. "Meet you over there."

Walking the main strip to the burger joint, I saw many bikes flying Old Glory. I knew this massive event stood for something bigger— freedom and rebellion, all wrapped up with a sense of belonging. Some clubs rode through town, but I didn't recognize any of them.

Bikes and bikers filled every patio, doorway, driveway, and sidewalk. I took it all in. These are my people. Todd and the guys talked hunting and family reunions while we ate. Fidgeting at the table, I decided to go for a walk. "Hey, I'm going to check out some of the shops. I'll be back in a few." My attention was fixated on all the men walking by. After checking out the antiques, leather goods, and the men wearing them, we continued our ride to the rally.

The bike barely came to a stop when I hopped off, stretching my legs while playing to the bikers admiring my skintight animal-print leggings and black leather halter. It resembled the leather vests my mother made for Jami and me when we were little. I took my leather-riding gloves off and tucked them into the saddlebag. I pulled on the slave bracelet my mother gave to me in high school. The ornate sterling silver piece had a cuff and a ring inlayed with black onyx, connected with beaded chains.

Memories of mom's belly-dancing classes in our living room came to mind. Her costume sparkled and jingled with ornamental jewelry, charms, and bells as she'd played her brass finger cymbals with her arms raised up at her side, shimmying her bare torso.

The dancers on the main stage of the Redwood Run wore far less. Many of the women left little to the imagination. Todd kept his arm around me while dodging the drunken crowd that ranged from respectable business owners to hard-core outlaw club members. The crowd went crazy when the band sang "Born to Be Wild."

Todd, his cousin, and brother-in-law gawked at the barely naked biker babes while I felt a bit tethered, unable to run wild. I moved in closer to my husband. I'm safe with Todd. Why would I want to go back to this and ruin everything we have? Todd's trustworthiness, respectfulness, and reliability opened my eyes to how much I was protected. He felt safe and kept me from falling into old behaviors.

My own father wasn't safe like Todd. He certainly didn't protect me. Even so, I missed him. Later that year, I invited my dad to join us for our first Thanksgiving in our new house. He and my stepmom made the two-hour trip for the holiday. They brought Jami and her boys, ages two and six with them. Dad couldn't wait to see the new bike. We all stood out front in the driveway of our modest track home as my dad looked it over. "Oh, it's one of them yuppie bikes," he joked with a sarcastic grin. Being an old-school biker didn't stop my dad from taking our shiny new bike for a spin when Todd offered him the key. The big Cheshire cat grin on Dad's face as he putted up the driveway said it all. He approved, and that's what mattered most.

My dad and Jami were close like I was to our mother. One could see it in his eyes when he watched Jami with his grandsons. Having babies came effortlessly for my sister. She often joked, "All I have to do is look at a guy and I get pregnant."

For whatever reason, she and our mother shared the same baby-making gene. I thanked God for protecting me from an unexpected pregnancy. There were a couple close calls, yet it never scared me into using birth control. At times, I wondered if I could even get pregnant.

Little did I know, the buried fear of never having children would soon be unearthed by an unexpected revelation that would reshape the course of my life.

Chapter 12

At the age of twenty-six, my biological clock ticked louder and more frequently with every baby shower I attended. The maternal side of me emerged for the first time. The longing for a child took me by surprise. With most of the girls at work starting their families, I did not want to miss out. I laughed off jokes about our drinking water at my office. "I'm Sicilian! We get pregnant when we open a bottle of vino!"

A visit to my OB/GYN revealed the inevitable. He deemed all the preliminary fertility tests unnecessary and scheduled an urgent HSG. The "slightly intrusive" hysterosalpingogram would determine abnormalities in and around the fallopian tubes and uterus.

The procedure took place an hour away from my doctor's office where his partner would perform the test. He briefed me on what to expect during the exam. A tall nurse wearing floral scrubs shut off the glaring overhead lights of the exam room. This helped the doctor view the intricate details on the ultrasound monitor. The nurse stood attentively at the side of the exam table while the doctor performed the procedure. Todd held my hand from the other side of the table. Severe cramping took my breath away. Our hope was for the bluish dye to move unrestricted through the fallopian tubes.

The doctor pointed out the various parts of my reproductive system on the ultrasound monitor. "See this? That's scar tissue. Your fallopian tubes and both ovaries are covered with it." He moved the pointer to my fallopian tubes, zooming in for a closer look. "And here your fallopian tubes are as big as my thumb. Horribly disfigured. They should be slim, like a pencil. It is obvious you've experienced trauma, along with silent infections. Were you sexually abused as a child?"

His demeanor mirrored the chill of the examination room, offering no solace for the anguish coursing through my veins. It wasn't just the acute, piercing pain of the catheter; it felt more like a deep, soul-wrenching agony. It tore at my heart, leaving behind a trail of bleeding hope and shattered purpose. In my dreams, I had envisioned a future with three children, a reflection of the family I had always longed for, just like my mom.

My words came out slow and soft. "Yes, I…I…yes."

He continued his cold clinical bedside manner. "Your infertility is not treatable. Unfortunately," he sighed, "the only way for you to conceive a child is through in vitro fertilization. And even that is experimental, with no guarantee." The doctor handed my chart to the nurse. I noticed her tears, offering comfort with a smile. "Peggy will give you all the details," he said, while exiting the exam room.

I lay, staring at the white ceiling tiles stained with neglect. Shock paralyzed my tear ducts. Nurse Peggy whispered, "I'll give you a few minutes alone." I asked her to leave the lights off.

I'd never felt so alone. Empty. Useless.

Todd's presence faded into the dimly lit room. Clenching my abdomen, the pressure of my rage erupted. "He stole my childhood! Now he gets to steal my motherhood too?"

Nurse Peggy returned with brochures and paperwork. Sobbing had to wait. Todd stood by my side while we learned about our options, either in vitro fertilization (IVF) or adoption. Viewing the damage to my reproductive system triggered another layer of trauma.

My husband helped me into the car. "Damn him to hell!" I sobbed. "Why me? How can Jami still pop out babies and I can't? I wonder how many other little girls he hurt. How could he do this to me? Evil. Pure evil." I took a deep breath and closed my eyes. I skated by since the age of twelve, messing around without getting pregnant. Am I being punished? Deep down, I knew this day would eventually arrive.

Todd started the car and we headed for our weekend destination at the coast. Seeking to offer support, my husband reached out and held my hand, his touch grounding me in the midst of turmoil. "Sweetheart, I married you for you. If we don't have children, I'm okay with that. With that said, I'll stand by you if this is something you really want."

The tears poured out. "I've always …" I tried to speak while searching my purse for a tissue. "I've always wanted three children. It was always what I saw happening. My mom had three kids."

In a matter of twenty-four hours, my existence and purpose shifted to starting a family. At that moment, nothing else held any significance. This new void catapulted me into unfamiliar territory.

Attending an orientation for IVF couples filled me with hope. Babies or infertility became inescapable. Four of my direct reports at work shared their own infertility struggles. Though our circumstances differed, we shared a heart for motherhood. Emotions raged during lunchroom conversations. Every baby shower invitation perpetuated my heartache.

When my mother suggested we take Grandma Mary to Mother's Day Brunch, I cringed. Why should I celebrate Mother's Day at all? Especially with my grandmother who bad-mouthed her own daughter. Choosing to not let her ruin our celebration. I conceded. Hmm…maybe this is just what I need. I'll announce our IVF plans to the whole family. This is the only way I can do this Mother's Day thing. I'll do it for Mom.

We met at my grandmother's favorite Chinese restaurant near her home in Saratoga. Generations of mothers waited with their families for a table. I took in the delicate beauty of the Chinese decor. My eighty-year-old grandmother sat between my mom and I at the large round table. Jami and her two boys joined us along with my brother and his two kids.

Our server poured a small amount of champagne into our crystal flutes. Grandma beamed with joy. She held her glass up to not be passed by. I figured it wouldn't be a problem to have a small taste. We laughed as we shared crazy stories from our childhoods.

I rested my hand on my grandmother's leg while clinging to my water glass. "Hey everyone, I have some exciting news." The chatter at the table stopped with all eyes turned toward me. "Todd and I are trying to have a baby. We're getting help from doctors, but we're doing it."

My family shared their cheers and wide-eyed congratulations. Grandma Mary shoved my hand away. In her gruff, drunken voice, she blared, "Baby! What the hell do you want to have a kid for?" she scowled. "They're no good."

In disbelief, I was at a loss for words. Couldn't she be happy for me? How could she say those things in front of her only child and generations of grandchildren? She continued her rant. I excused myself and ran to the restroom. Jami followed and attempted to comfort me with hugs and words that made sense.

"You know you can't listen to Grandma. You gotta let things roll off. I'm so happy for you guys. You're going to make the best mom."

To hear my sister's heartfelt words meant the world. I took the tissue she offered me, dabbing my eyes to keep from smearing my mascara. "I love you. Thank you. How can she be so mean? How can she talk about her own daughter that way ... and all of us?"

Jami took my hand. "C'mon, let's go back. Don't worry about Grandma. She drank too much champagne."

I straightened myself up. "You go ahead. I'll be right there." Mom may put up with her abuse, but I sure won't. I remembered when Mom mentioned her mother wanted her to abort me. Her comments about my dad. Her attitude about children. It all made sense now.

Jami switched chairs with me. But Grandma couldn't let it go. She leaned across Jami. "What are you so upset about?"

Jami cut her off with a hug. "Grandma, this is important to Cherie."

My grandmother shoved Jami away and took a swing at her. "Don't you touch me!"

I flew from my chair, shielding my sister. "Mom, it's time to leave. Get her out of here."

Discussing the logistics of IVF with my sister felt incredibly surreal. At one point, she offered to have a baby for me. Jami treasured the gift of motherhood and wanted to share it. Considering her ongoing struggle with drug addiction, drinking, and bulimia nervosa, I lovingly declined her offer.

What stood out more than anything was her unwavering love and her willingness to give me the gift of life. Jami loved her two boys.

She made it clear they were her lifeline, the one thing that gave her purpose and kept her going. Her relationships with their fathers were now in the past.

Jami's past two boyfriends were not much taller than her, which made it easier for her to defend herself. This time, she chose to marry someone over six feet tall, muscular, and covered in tattoos—one who got off on bruising and beating her fragile little body. I couldn't wrap my head around why she thought she had found a "real man".

When my mom told me about Jami's injuries, I promptly drove two hours to her house. I knocked repeatedly on the front door. Jami ignored me, but I didn't give up. She turned down her stereo, begging me to leave before her husband got home. "Go away, Cherie! You can't save me!"

With both hands placed flat on her door, I continued my plea. "No, but I can help you! Now, why don't you open the door?"

Jami tried to reason with me in a lower voice. "Look … I don't want to drag you in the middle of this. Please go! I'll be fine!"

With everything in me, I wanted to break that door down, pack her bags, and take her far away from that monster. My heart broke for her. I took several steps backward, holding out for Jami to change her mind. Sadly, she chose to stay.

The next morning, Todd and I signed paperwork with the fertility center. Then came the counseling. We talked to other couples who did IVF—some received a positive outcome, some didn't. On average, only one of three attempts proved successful. My health insurance did not cover the astronomical costs. We took a second mortgage on our house to cover the first cycle. Ordering fertility drugs from a French pharmaceutical company saved us a thousand dollars.

My workload already stretched my bandwidth and my mental capacity. Taking on the added financial burden concerned me. I found myself waking from nightmares again. Curled up in a fetal position one morning, I panicked. I can't do this. This is too much. What's wrong with me? How could I even think of taking this on right now?

In reality, we committed and there was no optimal time to begin our first IVF cycle. The fighter in me would not allow Van's evil to win this fight. When tragedy struck one of my coworkers, my doctor suggested we reconsider our timing. He said the added stress could throw the cycle off course. My assistant, Valerie, also struggled with infertility for several years. The drowning of her three-year-old miracle baby devastated all of us. I struggled over the correct path to take.

The decision to pursue this journey to motherhood required perseverance and possibly much more. When Monica invited me to the upcoming women's retreat with her church, I broke down on the phone with her. "I'm so glad you called. I can't get rid of this anger in me. I woke up to little demons jumping on my feet again. Everything around me is falling apart. Our business, my sister, and my friend's baby died. Plus, we're trying to have a baby. I feel guilty over that!" Monica listened to me pour my heart out to her. "I want what you have. I want it to be real. I think I need to go. Yes, I'll go."

My husband encouraged me to register for the Cathedral of Faith women's retreat. Despite my grief over Valerie's little girl, I now had the retreat to look forward to. Meanwhile, I tried to remain positive while starting the series of hormone injections. Blaming Van for the state of my health came too easy.

My doctor shared the encouraging news of our tremendous success with the harvesting of my eggs and the fertilization process. We followed the advice of our reproductive endocrinologist and implanted eight of the fifteen embryos. My body experienced every symptom of a pregnancy. A negative pregnancy test threw me for a loop.

The nurse explained the normalcy of a false sense of pregnancy with the hormone injections. I wished I'd known that beforehand. Todd never once complained about my radical mood swings or his duty of administering my shots. I experienced severe bruising on my stomach and hips from the daily injection throughout the thirty-day cycle. I felt like a pincushion. Tremendous guilt and shame tormented me.

Todd rolled with my emotional rollercoaster. At one of my lowest points, I nearly gave up while spilling my heart to him. "I'm so sorry, honey. I know you didn't sign up for this. Maybe I'm not supposed to have kids."

Speaking those words out loud sunk my heart deeper. Why are so many women clueless about the gift of life? I'd give anything to have the child my sister-in-law did not want. What worth is womanhood without the experience of motherhood?

I recalled the joy in the face of my coworkers when they shared about their babies. Their fulfillment compounded my emptiness. At the end of my rope, I hoped my time at the women's retreat would straighten out my life and rid me of the demons in my bed.

A couple girlfriends from work signed up too. Lisa and Julie were also Christians, but not to the extreme I saw in Monica. I hoped my expectations for the weekend were not unrealistic. Either way, I knew I'd need their support. During our drive to Mission Springs Christian Conference Center, Lisa encouraged me to take in each moment by moment. The drive over Highway 17 through the Santa Cruz mountains looked different in comparison to my previous trips.

We weren't heading for a beach weekend like the ones I remembered from my childhood. My anticipation grew stronger when Lisa took the Mt. Hermon Road exit. The entrance to the Mission Springs conference center appeared in the middle of the lush giant grove of redwood trees and surrounding mountain cabins. In more than twenty years of visiting this area, I never knew this magnificent place existed.

The three of us checked in at the registration desk. Monica met us there and introduced me to the sweetest ladies from her church. One lady with short grayish-blonde hair handed me a pretty gift bag. "We're so glad you're here, dear. Be sure to wear your bracelet and name tag throughout the weekend. God bless you."

After dinner, we gathered in the worship center which was similar to a large chapel. Behind the altar, a wall of windows reached the top of the vaulted beam ceiling. The display of the coastal giant redwoods outside the massive window stood as if to guard the sanctuary. They left me in awe as they climbed toward the sky.

The conference director, Lorraine Dennis, greeted the women from Cathedral of Faith, a large group of over three hundred attendees. With her silver curls and tailored light-blue outfit, the older woman exuded elegance. Her kind face lit up with a warm smile that instantly made you feel welcomed. After she led us in prayer, we sang with a woman who sounded like an angel.

The hymn, "Holy Ground," filled the sanctuary with a peaceful ambiance as it spoke of finding solace in Jesus. By the end of the night, I found myself caught between a web of questions and a sense of inner peace.

The sessions focused on anger and worry. I whispered to Lisa, "It's like she wrote her message for me." She smiled with a nod.

When Lorraine announced the time to share communion, I passed the basket filled with tiny pieces of bread to Lisa. She pushed it back my way. "Aren't you going to take communion?" I explained my experience when a Catholic priest told me I could not partake in communion. My friend assured me this was different. After receiving the bread and wine (grape juice), the worship leader sang another hymn. I rested my hands on the back of the pew in front of me. Every tear I cried felt like a release of everything bottled up inside me. I couldn't stop trembling. For one like me? I hoped those words she sang were true.

A soft touch on my shoulder felt so comforting. A woman with salt-and-pepper hair smiled and handed me a card with a note on it. "For I know the plans I have for you, says the Lord. They are plans for good and not for evil, to give you a future and a hope." (Jeremiah 29:11 TLB). I read it again. I furrowed my brow. How did she know of the evil in my life? That my plan to become a mother was troubling me?

Then, I understood. She shared a promise from God with me. This wasn't like opening a fortune cookie or reading a horoscope written by some fortune-teller. Taking in each word, one by one, I understood God gave me a special message. One that told me He had a better plan for my life. Good, not evil? What about Van? My grandfather? When I sensed the promise told of things to come, hope flooded my heart.

Our retreat director announced from the altar. "Now, if any of you ladies need special prayer, come on up. We don't bite." She laughed as she waved another one of the leaders over to join her.

I scooted to the edge of my seat, looking over at Lisa and Julie. "Let's go up," I urged.

They shook their heads. Lisa whispered, "Go on!"

It felt like my heart emitted a signal of distress, and somehow, God caught wind of my plea from heaven. Our speaker called me forward. I stumbled my way to the altar. I took my place in the line of several women. I closed my eyes and let the music soothe me. Longing welled up in my heart. Are you there, Jesus? I want to believe. I see what you did for Monica. I see, God. I believe. I do. It could only be you who stopped us nearly in midair from plunging down that canyon. Can you help me? I'm so afraid. I don't know what's wrong with me. Pain and shame flushed my face. I sensed a woman standing in front of me.

Her tender, compassionate voice whispered in my ear, "Oh, precious child. Jesus sees you. There is no need to hide your face in shame. You no longer need to run anywhere but into the arms of Jesus. He'll remove your pain." She placed her hand upon my forehead. "Are you ready to welcome Jesus as Lord of your life?"

Emptied, I pleaded, "Yes, I'm ready." I weakened with anticipation, fully surrendered to God's plan. I kneeled on the floor, reaching from my heart for Jesus. A beautiful melody filled the sanctuary as Donal, our worship leader, sang, "He touched me."

All the angst and rage left my soul. Peace flowed like I'd never known. Lying at the steps of the altar, opening myself up to Jesus, I continued to pray. He reminded me of the day I yelled out, "He stole my childhood. Now he gets to steal my motherhood?"

A stirring of peace brought words of comfort. I am a God of justice. Knowing God saw me and heard my cry that day amazed me. His response instilled the belief that He would not let evil prevail.

Chapter 13

The intense joy and excitement I felt consumed my conversations with friends and family. Upon returning to work, I shared my experience with one of my team members. He shared in my celebration and gave me a small devotional, My Utmost for His Highest, by Oswald Chambers. The tattered pages whispered stories of its cherished value to my friend.

Lisa told me she was rather shocked by my level of enthusiasm at the retreat. At work, nobody saw my vulnerable side, so that made sense.

Though I remained on what I described as a spiritual high, my newfound faith also brought confusion, and conflict. Since I found a church family at Cathedral of Faith, I began attending there every other week for their Sunday service. This thrilled my mom. She also enjoyed their worship and services.

Making the drive to San Jose every other week was no longer feasible after a few months. I set my heart on finding a local church exactly like Cathedral. Todd showed zero interest in joining me on my quest. One Sunday, I visited the largest church in the Sacramento area, which several friends recommended.

Not a single person welcomed me. That first impression kept me from staying until the end of the service. My friends at Cathedral of Faith always greeted people at the door with a smile and either a handshake or a hug.

The next church I visited exhibited the same poor hospitality. But that time, I sat front and center, ready to hear a message meant just for me. The pastor's sermon on forgiveness moved me to tears. I did not know how to deal with the anger and unforgiveness that created a storm in my soul. What I needed most was for someone to pass me a tissue, pray with me, or something. I got nothing. So, I didn't go back there either.

Attending church without my husband became lonely and challenging. He often argued that the Bible was only a book written by a group of men. I tried to describe to him how receiving Jeremiah 29:11 spoke directly into my soul.

Jami also turned down every invitation to go to church with me. Mom kept telling me how bad things were getting for Jami and asked me to pray for her. She flat-lined multiple times in the emergency room. Her cries echoed in my mind. You can't save me, Cherie.

But she survived, and I wanted more than anything for Jami to experience the peace I found. A deep urgency stirred within me to tell her about Jesus. I prayed every day, "Please, God. My sister needs you. Please help her."

The Lord heard my prayer and brought one of Jami's favorite recording artists, Peaches & Herb, to Cathedral of Faith. Though Jami seemed excited about the concert, she worried about what to wear. "All my clothes are black," she said, "and I can't wear black to church. Black is for funerals."

I sensed the devil holding her back. When I explained Jesus doesn't care what color she wears, Jami agreed to at least let me take her shopping. She picked out a cool pair of black pants and sweater.

The night of the concert, the youth choir started off the evening. One by one, the high school boys and girls filed out onto the stage. Half of the choir wore black, and the rest were in white. Jami nudged me with the biggest smile. We both were teary-eyed as the youth choir sang "Bridge Over Troubled Water." We knew God heard every word and showed up for her that night.

On our drive home, I brought it up. "You know how God arranged for you to see it doesn't matter what you wear to church?"

"Yes, can you believe that?"

"He did something like that for me at the retreat I went to. I never even prayed, and God knew exactly what I needed to hear. I've never felt such peace. Come with me next time, alright?" My heart filled with joy and surprise when she agreed.

Over the next few months, Todd and I committed to our next round of IVF. This time, we drove to Mexico to purchase my prescription drugs. I thought for sure we'd get arrested for smuggling a cooler filled with syringes across the border. We saved thousands of dollars by purchasing the medications there.

After enduring a demanding year of medical treatments and constant travel for work, the serene atmosphere of Mission Springs was a welcome respite upon my return. My deepest desire for Jami's deliverance and healing resonated in my heart. I reserved a room with four beds, envisioning Monica's prayers and words of encouragement for my sister. I tried to keep my excitement in check so I wouldn't freak out my sister, who clearly stepped out of her comfort zone.

The rustic barn-red lodge stood on the far side of a meadow nestled in the center of the grounds of the conference center. We climbed up the wooden stairs to the second level. I inhaled the fresh, coastal mountain air. We walked into the warm welcome of the room, brightly lit with the midday sun from the balcony window. I set my suitcase on the twin bed and checked out the bathroom. "Well, here we are. We certainly have plenty of room with four beds in here. Take your pick." I couldn't remember the last time we shared a bedroom. It must have been when we lived our father, more than a dozen years ago.

Jami fidgeted with her hands, biting her nails while peering over the balcony at the ladies arriving. "Wow, there's so many people here."

Remembering how out of place I'd felt last year, I let things take their course for her. No pushing. No planning. Despite her tough façade, I knew she hurt deep inside. God had a plan for her coming here, and I could not wait to see what that was.

Jami and I found Monica in the dining hall and ate with her and a few other ladies. I noticed Jami had already struck up a friendship with one of them. She joined us to reserve front seats before the worship center filled to capacity. Jami soaked in every word of the sessions. At times, she gave me a surprised and confused look while women cried in the sanctuary.

Back in our room, Jami asked. "Why is everyone crying?" She straightened her jacket, and, with a firm stance, she said, "I hope they don't expect me to cry. I don't cry."

I understood where she was coming from. "Nobody expects you to cry, but it is a safe place to let your emotions out and heal through your tears if you need to. Many of these women are crying because they are hurting. Others are crying because they feel the presence of God."

Raising her eyebrows and shaking her head, she said, "Well, I'm not crying."

Before turning in for the night, we wrote Bible verses on index cards. We discovered several beautiful promises. I chose Jeremiah 29:11, the verse given to me the previous year. Jami liked it and chose to use the same one.

Jami made a couple of friends while in the breakfast line the next morning. It made me smile. After worship, they announced we would take communion, but they were going to do something a bit out of the ordinary. We were asked to split up from whoever we were sitting with. Jami moved to the opposite side of the sanctuary. We exchanged our index cards we'd prepared the night before with the new person near us and served each other communion.

Jami called out across the sanctuary, waving her card in the air, and hurried toward me. "Oh my God! Cherie! You're not gonna believe what I got! My sister's tears took me by surprise. She handed me the green index card that read: "The righteous cry out, and the LORD hears them; He delivers them from all their troubles." (Psalm 34:17 NIV)

Jami shared how she cried to God many times while journaling her prayers. Jami sobbed while recounting her decision to never cry out to Him again. She figured, what's the point?

I held her. We cried tears of joy together for the first time. Jami had finally heard from the Lord. All the while, God seemed to know the plan and how this weekend would play out. She welcomed Jesus into her life, and many witnessed an immediate change in her countenance.

That night, Jami shared lyrics to Suicidal Failure, a song she declared as her life anthem. My heart hurt for her, recognizing how long the devil tormented her with the desire to end her life. She stood, speaking with a strength I'd never seen in her. "I've been singing this song to myself for a long time. But you know what? I don't feel like that anymore."

When my tears cleared, I asked her to write the words down on paper. I tucked the piece of paper into my pocket. Guilt and shame washed over my heart like a tidal wave. I wish I could have protected her. I wish I would have treated her better. I wish my life wasn't so much better than hers. Why didn't I do more for her? Why did she have to suffer so much more than me?

During our last session, Lorraine announced we would have a foot-washing. Our retreat leader described foot-washing as a ritual of humility, mirroring Jesus's act of washing His disciples' feet.

Kneeling before her, I covered Jami's bare feet with warm water. From my anguished heart, I prayed, "Lord, please forgive me. Forgive me for treating my sister so badly when we were young. Please forgive me for not keeping her from harm. Jesus, give her peace."

My tears fell over the top of her feet. Weeping, I heard deep in my soul: Look what you are doing now. You brought her to Me. In an instant, a deep calmness swept through my soul.

When I looked at my sister's face, I saw her in a whole new way—as a precious child of God. I believed God blessed me with the gift of seeing her through His eyes. His love enveloped me. I thanked Him for orchestrating our time alone in our room. He knew rooming with others would hinder Jami from opening her heart to me. He may have brought us together to shower His beloved daughters with His love, but He also reconciled and healed our sister-hearts.

At breakfast on our last day of retreat, I caught Lorraine and shared the significance of the weekend's impact on Jami. I gave her the piece of paper onto which Jami wrote out the song lyrics. Lorraine began to read the words, then swiftly folded up the white ruled paper into a small square and slipped it into her sweater pocket. Lorraine tried to smile behind tears. "My dear, thank you for pulling me aside to share this. We'll pray over Jami before we wrap up."

When our closing session commenced, we took our seats at the front of the worship center. Following the session, Lorraine and the co-director, Barbara Donaldson, led us in prayer. Both women stood at the podium which was carved from redwood. Lorraine unfolded the paper and placed it in a bowl. The previous night, Barbara had been seated next to Jami in the front pew and talked with her for awhile. With a gentle touch and a loving call, Barbara extended her hand towards my sister. "Jami, dear child, would you come up?

Jami turned to me with a look of surprise, shrugging her shoulders. She did not hesitate and walked up the steps to the altar. Barbara hugged her and asked Jami to stand between her and Lorraine.

Lorraine tore the paper into tiny pieces at the pulpit and surrendered the lyrics to God. Lorraine and Barbara prayed over Jami with their hands on her forehead and shoulders. "Jami, I declare these words will no longer have any power over your life." Are you ready to accept Jesus Christ as Lord over your life?"

Jami fought her tears and nodded. "Yes, I am."

Everyone in the sanctuary stood, applauding, and praising Jesus for saving Jami. And to seal her incredible time at the retreat, Jami recognized one of the ladies as a singer she admired greatly. She was in disbelief that this person would ever 'come to something like this.'

Jami could not contain the fire burning in her heart once she left the mountaintop. The following weekend, Jami took her husband and two young boys to Cathedral of Faith, where they all welcomed Jesus into their hearts.

Jami began making amends and reconciling broken relationships, telling everyone about Jesus. But her body remained weak from the damage already caused by drug addiction, acute asthma, and bulimia.

Weeks later, my travels resumed. I sat in the front of a conference room at the World Council of Credit Unions in Chicago. Familiar faces from previous conferences occupied the room. Chatter ensued among the attendees. The presenter peeked from the doorway and whispered, "Excuse me, are you Cherie?"

I nodded and walked toward the door.

"You have a phone call," he said, handing me the phone. "You can take it out here in the hall. It sounds urgent."

I clasped my chest to brace myself and put the receiver to my ear. It was Todd. He asked me if I was alone. I leaned into the wall. Todd strained to get the words out. "There's been an accident. It's Jami."

His pause elevated my heart rate. I paced the hall. "Oh no!" I whispered. "Is she okay? What happened?"

"Honey, they tried … umm … she didn't make it. I'm so sorry. Your mom was by her side when she passed."

My insides tightened into a ball. I couldn't believe it and cried, "What?" You're saying Jami died? What?" Dazed, I held my hand on my head. I looked around for someone. "I have to get home. I have to get to my mom."

Those seven hours on the plane felt more like seventy hours. Sobbing through my prayers led to replaying our time together at the retreat like a movie reel. This is it? How could she be gone so quick? This wasn't how I pictured it. What about her boys? How do I tell them You are good when their mother died immediately after trusting you? What now? Their poor little hearts.

The travel time helped me work through the shock. I tried to make sense of Jeremiah 29:11 and Psalm 34:17. Both verses promised to protect her from evil.

Todd drove me to Manuel's, where my mother now lived. With barely enough strength to speak, my mom told me Jami died while running across the Almaden Expressway trying to catch a bus. A young man driving a van hit her.

Mom also revealed that through Jami's recent series of hospital stays, Jami's doctor alerted her to the severity of her health and the irreversible damage to her body. He estimated she might only live a few more months. God allowed me to see His purpose with a moment of clarity. He knew the suffering Jami would endure in the upcoming months. He wanted her to know Him intimately. He whood her with His love. And then her babies. Thank you, Jesus, for rescuing her from further suffering. You knew she suffered enough. Jesus heard her cries. He saw her struggle. He delivered her from all of her troubles, just as He promised.

In my grief, knowing this enabled me to celebrate at her memorial. All of us celebrated Jami's homegoing to Jesus with one of her favorite songs from the retreat. This is the day the Lord has made. Let us rejoice and be glad in it. I prayed our parents would understand that perspective one day. Monica stood by our family and helped us pull the memorial and burial together. Manuel made sure everything was paid for. Because of recovering from major heart surgery, our father waited in his van in the parking lot of the memorial chapel. Jami's boys, aged four and eight, were just starting to learn about Jesus. They knew nothing of death. I wanted to help them learn it was okay to celebrate their mom going to heaven.

My mother mentioned receiving a call that her brother, Barry, planned on attending. As far as anyone knew, he was still serving a prison sentence. Seconds after Barry pulled up to the front of the chapel, FBI agents tackled him on the ground with shotguns drawn. I motioned for everyone else to hurry and get inside. The ordeal was insane, but typical of our family.

Lorraine adored Jami and agreed to officiate her memorial service. Barbara Donaldson also joined us. When all the commotion broke out, Lorraine told me, "Cherie, this is how the devil works. He thinks he's going to keep these young people from Jesus."

Barbara shared with the standing-room-only crowd the hope my sister found in Jesus. Members of the youth choir, both dressed in black, sang "Bridge Over Troubled Water."

More than twenty of Jami's friends committed their life to the Lord that day. Just as we celebrated on earth, Jami surely rejoiced in heaven.

Chapter 14

Losing my sister shattered our family. Jami's boys lived with my mother for a short while until each of them ended up going to live with their respective fathers. The tragedy of losing their mother and then one another seemed unbearably cruel to me.

As the only family member with a glimmer of faith, I clung to it like a life preserver. My mom needed comfort through her unbearable grief, but I could only do so much. When I spent time with her, I noticed her obsession with miniature doll houses. My mother's child-like state helped her cope with her grief. She refused to attend grief counseling. When I mentioned it, she'd tell me it hurts too much to talk about it.

I knew the nineteen-year-old man who struck Jami must also be suffering. I wanted more than anything to reach him. My heart hurt for him. He must know he is not to blame, and we understand this was a horrific accident. When I contacted the police department, they refused to release his contact information. The officer found it suspect that I would want to communicate with him. All I could do was pray for the young man.

I continued to go to God about many things. After consulting with my doctor, we put our IVF plans on the back burner until I felt ready to return to the regimen of poking and prodding. Plus, Todd and I needed time to put money aside for it.

Meanwhile, Laurie, a coworker, announced her success with her first round of IVF. She celebrated the news of being blessed with triplets. To her dismay, one weak heartbeat could potentially threaten the survival of the other two fetuses. I could not imagine the turmoil she endured when her doctor suggested she must deaden the weaker heartbeat.

Another coworker, Melanie, went the adoption route. She and her husband finally brought home their newborn little boy, only for the birth mom to change her mind five months later.

The loss of life … of dreams … sent me spinning. I realized if God meant me to have a child, it would happen … in His time. Managing my stress challenged my faith.

I gave up my search for a church that fit all my requirements and my visits to Cathedral became less frequent. However, on one Sunday, the pastor announced the upcoming women's retreat. Mom wanted to join me. Monica could not stop talking about the keynote speaker. Stephanie Boosahda apparently possessed a special spiritual gift that allowed her to receive and relay divinely inspired messages to others in the church.

I arrived without seeking or expecting anything for myself. I entered the worship center, thinking "I want my mom to encounter Jesus. I want to pray for all the women who prayed over us the past couple of years."

Over three hundred women were quickly filling up the sanctuary. I held my mother's hand and looked for a seat near the entrance. I asked, "Is this okay?" I did not want the attention on me. We took our seats in the last row, and I closed my eyes. Oh, Lord, please comfort my mother. She's dying inside, God.

Before Stephanie began, she spoke God's blessing over all of us. I rested my head on the back of the wooden pew in front of me and prayed along. The weight of all the suffering and heartache my family and I had endured crushed my heart. Grief-fueled tears poured out.

Stephanie continued, "There is a woman in the room who is barren. Your organs … your organs are damaged, keeping you from having a child." She continued the detailed description. I cried and prayed for another woman in the room. I could relate to her.

My mother grabbed my hand, raised it up, and stood. She shouted, "It's my daughter! It's my daughter!"

Startled, I looked up. Stephanie held her arms over the crowd, prophesying. She moved from the altar down the middle of the room toward us. "My child, stand up." She looked right at me. "Come up. Come up here with me."

My mother nudged me to go forward for prayer.

I hesitated. *It can't be my turn again, Lord. It must be someone else.*

Stephanie ushered me to the front pew, the spot I purposely decided against sitting in this year. I told her about my infertility journey, which confirmed her prophetic prayers. Lorraine and Stephanie placed their hands on my abdomen and the top of my head and prayed for the devil to get away from me.

Although the experience was new and strange, I was all in. My stomach and body trembled. Doubt and fear left my mind. Peace and trust in God's promises replaced the lies and deception I carried. I now believed God would entrust me with a child. Gathering myself on the steps of the altar, incredible peace consumed me.

My priorities changed. Todd's new job working in underground construction allowed me to step down from my management role. In retrospect, I made a huge mistake in leaving the credit union altogether. Instead, I took a part-time administrative position with a much smaller credit union. With the weight of work-related stress lifted, I found myself in a more peaceful state of mind while preparing for the third IVF attempt.

I knew it would be a success. I did my part and trusted God. When the doctor confirmed my pregnancy, Todd and I celebrated. God did not allow the devil to steal my motherhood.

When I showed up at the next women's retreat five months later, everyone praised God and celebrated with me. Most women guessed me to be much further along. Some even suspected twins. What a joy for all those ladies to witness the answer to their prayers for my baby. I belonged there. I was home at Mission Springs with all these incredible women. My sweet friends prayed over my baby girl on the very altar where I'd stood the past three years, receiving miracle after miracle.

Once I felt my baby kick, I began reading Bible stories to her every morning and evening while rocking in the chair set up in her nursery. Todd scoffed at me one night, saying the baby couldn't hear me. I argued, "Why wouldn't she hear me? She's inside my body." I realized then he didn't get it. I nurtured every step of her development with my nutrition. Why wouldn't I nurture her spiritually?

With only six weeks to term, my doctor estimated my baby girl already weighed nine pounds. The pressure on my short frame made it difficult to stand long enough to brush my teeth.

On New Year's Eve, I asked Todd to cancel his weekend plans. He worked on a pyrotechnics crew on the side and the team had to set up for the biggest show of the year at a ski resort at Lake Tahoe's North Shore. I pleaded with my husband, "What if something happens? I have no way to reach you." I grew anxious, realizing he would be a couple hours away.

We argued in the garage while he packed his things. Supporting the weight of my baby girl with my hands, I leaned against the car. The tearing and stretching sensation around my womb worsened.

In a calmer state, I gave it one last shot. "You know, I really would like it if you could stay home with me. I'm not feeling so good." Crying from excruciating pain, I begged, "Please don't go."

My husband barely looked at me. He said emphatically, "Steve is expecting me to be there. Your mom is here if you need anything. I'll see you in two days."

When I watched him back the car out of the driveway, I stood in disbelief. My tears stopped the moment the taillights disappeared from sight. He didn't even kiss me. I married the wrong man.

For the first time in ten years, I questioned the security I'd found with my husband. Memories of rejection, abandonment, and unworthiness consumed me. I thought I could trust him. He's supposed to protect me. How could he leave like that?

A month later, I gave birth to my daughter two weeks early, by C-section. Angelica weighed more than ten pounds. My marriage grew more strained over the next few months. No matter how hard I tried, I couldn't escape the deep-seated mistrust I felt toward Todd.

New Year's Eve was like a never-ending loop. Hunting and fishing trumped all family events, even attending our best friend's wedding together. His disdain for my family caused more distance. I almost gave up on asking Todd to join me for church.

But one weekend, I gave it one last shot. Todd agreed to check out Cathedral of Faith. In my excitement, I phoned Lorraine to ask if we could connect after the service. She knew of the struggles in our marriage.

Following the service, Lorraine prayed over us in the courtyard behind the church. She pointed out two doves perched above us in the cherry blossom tree. In her sweet voice, she said, "They symbolize the Holy Spirit."

Todd and I prayed together at home that night, but I sensed insincerity. I'm sure he prayed to indulge me. In the coming weeks, he appeased me with suggestions to read the Bible together. When he mentioned praying or reading together, I sensed manipulation.

He confirmed my doubt by disrespecting me in front of family. The loathing tone in his voice and his looks of disgust stayed with me. When Angelica discovered her voice, she began picking up on Todd's sarcastic tone toward me. The bond between Todd and I faded, leaving us emotionally detached. He told me he found forty acres in the northeast corner of California for us to build a home on. I'm not sure what would make him think I'd move that far away from civilization or our family. I think I told him he could go by himself.

In the weeks following, I had a vivid dream that was unlike anything I had ever experienced. The scene appeared with us driving around an island, like Hawaii. Todd sat in the passenger seat. I sensed we were vacationing because he smiled while looking for a place to explore. A blanket of fog blew across the highway. I strained to see the road but continued driving. The fog thickened by the minute. With zero visibility, I pulled to the side of the highway to let my husband take the wheel. But, when Todd stepped from the truck, he plummeted down the embankment. Panic struck me, jolting me awake.

At the time, I never considered the devil's attempt to steal, kill, and destroy everything good in my life. Later, I discovered how the enemy manipulated me through online chat rooms, creating a false sense of emotional support. The online frenzy reeled me in. Chat room conversations led to one-on-one conversations.

Todd questioned my late nights on the computer. His suspicions confirmed with an email from a man who wanted to rendezvous. Todd began writing me love notes and bringing me flowers. Unfortunately, I no longer trusted or respected him. His futile attempts to reverse the damage to our marriage only caused greater distance between us.

The memory of my husband choosing to abandon me on New Year's Eve, when I needed him the most, only intensified the bitterness and unforgiveness in me. That betrayal acted as a catalyst, reigniting my desire to find protection and belonging elsewhere. Returning to those familiar coping mechanisms distanced me from God and ended my marriage.

Our family and friends were shocked on so many levels. In their eyes, Todd and I were the storybook husband and wife. Cindy understood the heartache I suffered and had witnessed our conflict, firsthand. One friend completely cut ties with me for years, accusing me of having a tendency to overreact to things. What made our divorce the worst possible choice, in her eyes, was the thought of the lasting impact it would have on our daughter.

Some friends and family chose a side, while others opted for complete detachment. In short, the aftermath of our divorce was far-reaching. Todd's behavior following the divorce filing grew bizarre and scared me. He pleaded for reconciliation. He stalked me from outside my bedroom window. Part of his stalking and narcissistic behavior included coercing a mutual friend into stealing papers from my purse. I would never understand the purpose behind Todd wanting my DMV paperwork.

At thirty-four, I struggled to make it on my own. I did not know how to live alone, and my emotional state made it difficult to maintain stability with my work. People I'd befriended throughout my career, who I considered family, were not there for me.

During this time, I learned about relational dynamics. Not all friends had my best interest at heart. Some were there only to benefit in some way, but once my life derailed, they disappeared. I did not have a tribe of girlfriends or a community of any kind.

Todd's manic behavior made coping more difficult. During Todd's parenting days, relentless waves of loneliness and despair often brought me to the floor. Shame consumed me for allowing the generational cycle of divorce to continue. I beat myself up instead of turning to God.

To cope, I chased after sex. Sex became an act, void of any emotion. The online chat rooms lured me, creating endless opportunities to meet men. I could now grasp my mother's wild years of dating following her divorce. Only, with current technology, I could hide behind a computer screen, along with the rest of them.

The number of cheating husbands I talked to surprised me. For some twisted reason, I considered them safe. I encountered countless life-threatening situations, and I'm still amazed I survived.

An empty shell, I found my worth in the physical desire I received from those who were most unworthy of me. One guy I'd been chatting with online for a couple of weeks asked me to meet him for dinner. When I showed up at the abandoned restaurant, I knew I had to get out of there.

Only God could have spared my life that night.

Chapter 15

Despite the dangers of the online social scene, I continued searching for connection to the biker world. The discovery of biker chats excited me. They are the only ones I can trust. They will protect me. I'm home with them. I know how to be a good biker's ole lady. It's in my blood. Memories of the Redwood Rally convinced me that true belonging meant fully embracing my biker bloodline.

One biker I connected with online introduced me to his girlfriend. Penny rode her own motorcycle and worked nearby. She and I met up for a drink and hit it off. Penny and her ole man invited me everywhere. I didn't mind riding on the back of her boyfriend's bike once in a while. They were into sex parties and often invited me to events at the local Hells Angels clubhouse. Sexual confusion challenged my beliefs. I loved men and had no desire to adopt a bisexual lifestyle. Penny always had my back, regardless of my choices.

Another biker I met invited me to the largest Toys for Tots ride in the State of California. Dean rode with the Legacy Vets, a sister club to the Vietnam Vets Motorcycle Club (VNVMC). Though Dean was still a Prospect, the rest of the brothers showed him great respect. Dean served in the U.S. Air Force Reserve six months out of the year. Club members always had a road name like Knuckles or Road Dog sewn into a patch on their cut. When I asked Dean to explain how he came up with "Word" for a road name, he explained his club brothers came up with it because of his use of fancy words in the club's newsletter. I loved that we both shared a passion for writing.

Word and I became official and began seeing each other. One night, he picked me up from my house on his Harley-Davidson Dyna Low Rider. He couldn't wait to show me off to the club. When we pulled up to the Tumbleweed Bar, a dive biker bar, more than a hundred motorcycles packed with stuffed animals and toys overflowed the parking lot. I felt a sense of pride while riding through downtown Sacramento to the state capitol. The Marine Corps facilitated the historical Toys for Tots toy drive, collecting toys for children who would not otherwise have a Christmas. Thousands of bikers from all over the state paraded around the city.

Back at the Tumbleweed, Word introduced me to everyone as his lady. When he put his arm around my shoulders, I knew I belonged to him. Word's six-foot-four-inch frame made me, at five-foot-two, feel secure.

The bartender served us our drinks and winked at me. "It's a pleasure to meet you, lovely lady."

Word smiled and raised his glass. "She's a good girl, Larry."

The women welcomed me like a sister. One of them complimented me for taking him off the market.

One Sunday, Word told me his mom invited us over for her famous enchiladas. I thought it meant a lot for him to invite me to his mother's house. I arranged for my daughter to spend the night with her dad. That night, Word showed me pictures of women with tattoos and said how beautiful they looked. The next time I saw him,

I modeled my new body art, a colorful tribal vine with peacock feathered leaves circling my chest.

My self-sabotage did not stop there. When Word ditched me on the afternoon of the Valentine's Day Sweetheart Run, I snapped. I could not conceive of any man preventing me from riding again. So, one day at work, while reconciling the corporate bank account, I embezzled enough money to purchase a bike of my own.

I called Penny to help me get it home. After a few weeks of practice, I showed up at The Tumbleweed on a new Harley Davidson. A few of the VNVMC brothers stood out front around the bikes. The sight of a woman riding up on a new Harley caught everyone's attention. I received plenty of stares while I parked beside the dozen other Harleys. The sight of Word's jaw dropping when I removed my helmet was truly priceless.

Word stepped closer and questioned me. "I knew you loved to ride…but this? How did you come up with this windfall of money?" His warning not to do anything to jeopardize my daughter came too late. I did what I had to do to belong, and I left that temporary job shortly after.

The Memorial Day ride, the mother of all gatherings, brought VNVMC chapters from all around the country. The Prospects from the local VNVMC chapter set up at one of the nearby VFW grounds. They'd host the guest chapters arriving throughout the week. A prospect such as Word remained at the beck and call of every patch holder on the premises. Regardless of the circumstances, if a full-patch member needed something, Word had to be prepared to respond. Club members, whether patched or not, considered every patch holder family and held a higher position than one's own blood relatives. Being part of this initiation was a significant milestone for the prospect on his path to becoming a patch holder. I did not understand these things growing up around Little Joe and the Warlords. The rest of us laughed hysterically watching the group of prospects singing "Stand by Your Man" gathered around the bonfire.

The next morning, the club brothers discussed our ride to the California Vietnam Veterans Memorial. More than one hundred motorcycles, with the brothers flying colors of red and black, took their position. I rode alongside Word toward the rear of the pack. The brothers proudly flew the American and POW flags.

While we rode in formation on the freeway to the California State Capitol, cars moved over, clearing the way for us. Drivers honked their horns to show solidarity and support for the men riding their motorcycles along the highway, while also paying tribute to those they were riding for. A sense of reverence and honor flooded my heart for these warriors.

Attending the Memorial Day ceremony at the Vietnam Veterans Memorial with them opened my eyes to much more. The brothers walked quietly with honor up to the memorial wall to locate the names of their fallen brothers. Their stories of war and loss penetrated my heart. Deep sorrow, compassion, and grief overwhelmed me to the point of tears. After that day, I wanted nothing more than to remain among them. I'll prove myself worthy. I found my people.

Spending time with the club gave me a boost. But Word stopped calling me. He thought I'd run off like a rejected puppy dog. By this time, though, I had befriended many brothers and sisters from various local clubs. And with a bike to ride, I waited around for nobody.

When the VNVMC chapter president, Batman, invited me to join them on a weekend run to the coast, I was elated. We started with the blessing of the bikes. The club chaplain prayed over every rider and their bike. The chaplain made his way around the bikes, beginning with the officers and working his way down the ranks to the prospects.

When the chaplain prayed over brother Half Ton, I felt a stirring in my soul. My heart broke for him as I recalled a recent conversation with him about the loss of his wife and daughter in a car crash. The chaplain discerned the tremendous grief Half Ton carried in his heart when he said, "Brothers, you have a special man here."

I nodded. I knew it too. They were all heroes in my book. The question of faith weighed heavily on my mind, both for the brothers and for myself.

We rode Highway 1 north along the California coast to a hidden grove of redwoods on forty acres and set up camp. I picked a spot tucked in the trees away from the others and unpacked my bike. Half Ton wandered off by himself. I wanted to hang out with him, but I did not want anyone to get the impression we were together. Though one of the club officers chaperoned me along the ride, I camped alone.

I walked the property with some of the other sisters. Audrey, a statuesque blonde in her mid-twenties, belonged to Tony, one of the other chapter presidents. The scowl on Tony's face told me he didn't care for her taking off with me. We walked across the property in our tight leather pants and low-cut tops. Surrounded by a few hundred sex-crazed bikers, I felt their eyes follow us. One of the prospects approached us at the beer garden. "Audrey, I am here to tell you to get back to camp. Tony isn't happy."

We didn't dare say anything. My new friend looked down and shook her head in frustration. With a shrug and roll of the eyes, she set her beer down. "Guess I'll catch ya later, girl." She sighed with disdain.

I'd never seen one of the sisters treated like that before. Little John, a VNVMC officer, gave his ole lady, Tammy, much more freedom. Little John got his name from Little John in The Three Musketeers.

Tammy, Little John, and I waited in line for some bottled water when one of the patch holders approached me. "Hey, gorgeous. Maybe we could do some dancing when the music starts!" He wrapped his arm around my neck. I pulled away, though I didn't want to make him mad.

Tammy spoke up. "Hey, Ice. I don't think that's a good idea. You know, she rode up here with Danny."

He stepped back. "Danny, huh?" He lifted both arms away from me. "Well, let me know if you change your mind."

It took me a second to process what happened. I appreciated Tammy's intervening. I looked down and shuffled my boot in the dirt. "Uh, thank you for that."

Tammy chuckled. "No problem. He's the last guy you need bothering you. Stick close to us."

I knew Tammy and Little John from parties at the Devil's Horsemen's clubhouse in south Sacramento. Little John was also an officer of the VNVMC and Word's assigned patch holder. For whatever reason, Word did not join them this weekend, which made things better for me.

The Too Much Fun Club (TTMFC is a real biker club) knew how to throw a party. They set up an enormous grill with a wide variety of meat and seafood. Billy Idol, a member of TTMFC, performed live for us. People handed me shots of tequila while dancing to "White Wedding," one of Idol's popular songs.

Each time I staggered back to the VNVMC camp, I grabbed a seat at the campfire next to Batman. He insisted. I lost count of the party balloons passed my way, inflated with some sort of psychotropic drug. I inhaled six or more.

The flames from the fire heated my face, and my head spun. I stood up to find the bathroom. I felt as light as a feather, like a gust of wind could have toppled me. I found the makeshift bathroom-slash-outhouse after wandering in circles around the outbuilding.

A prospect from another VNVMC chapter startled me when I came out of the bathroom. I recognized Dave from a party at The Tumbleweed. He wrapped his arms around my shoulders. "I thought I'd make sure you get to your tent safely."

I never made it back to join Batman at the campfire. I don't even remember passing out in my tent. What I do know is I awoke to the cold steel of a .45 pressed against my skin—Dave slept with it between our pillows.

A few of the sweet girls I met made a living dancing in strip clubs. Giving every worthless piece of myself away provided a twisted sense of acceptance and belonging. I even tried to join the Devil Dolls, the all-girls version of the Hells Angels. They could ask me to do anything, and I'd do it, no problem.

A few months later, at a Halloween bash, one of the Misplaced Souls brothers stopped me from entering a wet T-shirt contest. He grabbed my hand. "Cherie, you're not like those girls. You don't belong up there."

I put the pen down and stood there, bewildered.

"We don't want girls like that," he said. "You're an incredible woman. Look at yourself that way."

I didn't see myself that way. All I wanted was to be one of those ladies with a property patch. But I wanted them to include me like one of the guys. I became close friends with some of the MMA officers and helped them with their newsletter. They were tight with the Hells Angels, and I appreciated keeping them close. I knew only one other sister who rode her own bike.

A few of the club sisters and I did our duty and went to the polls on election day. Afterward, we went for a round of drinks. That's the day I met Lefty. He sat alone at the opposite end of the bar. I felt his eyes on us, and I looked over. I asked the bartender to include him in our next round of drinks. He nodded his long grayish blonde locks of hair and raised his shot glass. Two weeks later, Lefty asked me out.

We met back at the little biker bar. Lefty stood about six feet tall in his black denim pants, white T-shirt, and leather motorcycle boots. His rather decorative brown leather vest, trimmed in black braided leather, did not resemble the cuts worn by the bikers I knew. But I still liked his flowing silver locks and long silver goatee, offset by the intensity of his blue eyes.

When we took our seat at the bar, he pulled out pieces of paper from the inside pocket of his vest. He unfolded them and said he'd like to share some of his poetry with me. Being a writer myself, I admired his vulnerability. Lefty suggested we go to the back of the room, away from the pool tables and the crowded bar area. He told me to stand facing the large decorative mirror on the wall. There, he proceeded to read his poems with tremendous emotion. Lefty's words moved me to tears. This guy is sentimental. He's experienced so much pain in his life.

When he confessed he did not know how to ride a motorcycle, I thought he was kidding around. Over time, I taught him how to ride. My heart did not see it at the time, but the devil snuck in and used Lefty to seduce me.

Amid everything, I struggled to keep the bank from foreclosing on my house. Todd fought against me on every financial matter and refused to provide child support. When he sabotaged my daycare arrangements, I had no choice but to quit my job. I couldn't cope.

After a friend told me about a job opportunity with the State of California, I tested and scored in the ninety-eighth percentile. Now, I'd wait to wade through all of the red tape. Until then, I began working temporary assignments through an employment agency. I could not pull the finances together to keep my house, so I had no option but to let it go in a short sale. Another blow. Another failure. More loss.

Todd decided to play hard ball and opened a case with the family law court. He intended to move out of state. I knew of his plan to take our daughter with him. Angelica wanted to stay with her father more often. They lived with his mother, so Angelica became close to her nana. Unfortunately, her nana now refused to watch Angelica after school during my parenting days. Todd sabotaged all the support systems I established in an effort to prove me an unfit mother.

I stayed with a girlfriend around the corner for a few months until I could secure an apartment close to Angelica's school. Like clock-work, I'd wake up at 3:00 most mornings with my mind racing. I wrote it off to stress. I'd usually make myself a cup of tea and go back to sleep. But one night I dreamed of a day of celebration. I saw my mother standing next to a man in a tuxedo. They were getting married. I sat on the edge of a patio table, swinging my bare feet. Before the ceremony, the groom turned his head toward me. The rough, aged character of my father's face emerged within a blurred haze of light. Looking me square in the eyes, in an audible voice, he said, "Tell them ... Romans 10."

I woke from the dream. Tell them? Tell them what? Romans 10? That sounds like something from the Bible. Searching through boxes for my Bible, I repeated the words. I'd never read the book of Romans. I flipped through the pages. I laughed and thought I didn't get a simple verse, but a whole chapter.

I read the entire book. Romans 10:13-15 (NLT) struck my heart. "Everyone who calls on the name of the LORD will be saved. But how can they call on him to save them unless they believe in him? And how can they believe in him if they have never heard about him? And how can they hear about him unless someone tells them? And how will anyone go and tell them without being sent?"

I sat on the edge of my bed, shaking my head in awe.

This is a message straight from God.

Chapter 16

The following year, my crime caught up with me. The police confiscated my motorcycle from Lefty's house while I was at work. Lefty received the call from his son. A wave of dread washed over me, signaling the impending chaos that was about to consume my world. That warning from Word echoed in my mind: Don't do anything to jeopardize your daughter.

Too late now. I would meet with the district attorney to discuss the allegations. My thoughts wreaked havoc inside. I wanted to be a part of the family. No. Be honest with yourself, Cherie. You thought you could get away with it. The realization that I had stolen the motorcycle was inescapable. Even negotiating my way out would not prevent the district attorney from moving forward with charges of felony grand theft.

The scene in the office reminded me of an interview panel, except I jeopardized my freedom. I could not lose the only thing that mattered—my daughter. Intimidated and scared, I pleaded, "I'll do whatever it takes to work off what I owe. Please give me the chance to make things right."

The DA suspected that I might be colluding with the maintenance manager, who was alleged to have stolen dental equipment worth over a quarter million dollars. As I spoke, I felt the weight lift off my shoulders, knowing I had no knowledge about that.

On the way to my first court hearing, I read the obituaries. I wasn't sure why, as I never read the obituaries. One of my friends died in a senseless bicycle accident when he collided with a car head on. My heart deflated, I read on … and read about the death of the dentist I stole from. He wanted to help me make good on my crime. He told me he believed me about wanting to make things right, but it was out of his hands at that point.

A lump formed in my throat. Now he's gone? God, what does this mean? Did I kill him?

Angelica, now in third grade, grew more distant from me. After Red Ribbon Week at her school, she came home and asked if I was a drug addict. Apparently, drinking beer raised a red flag in her eyes. She wanted me to stop, so I respected her wishes.

My angel babe possessed wisdom beyond her years. Her relationship with her father grew stronger because of her disapproval of my biker lifestyle. The loss of our home hurt her terribly. I also introduced her to a dangerous world, the same biker culture I ran from myself. The fallout of my actions was inevitable. And now, due to my job issues, I had no choice but to move in with Lefty.

I reflected on my accomplishments throughout my life. But now … how did any of that matter? The catastrophic consequences of my actions left me feeling helpless while my life spun further into chaos. A huge encouragement was I finally landed in the job queue with the State of California. My test score of ninety-eight percent resulted in a flood of job opportunities—up to a dozen applications arrived in my mailbox in one week.

Having the upper hand to choose which position to pursue felt empowering. Holding a secretarial position with the Department of Health and Human Services worked to my advantage in my family court case. I could also dig myself out of my financial mess.

But then came the morning of my sentencing. My ex-husband sat smugly in the back of the courtroom with his sister by his side, ready to pounce. His scumbag lawyer already promised to take my daughter away from me forever. Fortunately, I found other living arrangements, renting a room with an old friend. I wore my office attire and kept my emotions intact.

"Miss LaLanne," the judge said with a tone of compassion, "the district attorney typically requests a sentence of up to one year in prison for a crime like this. Since you do not have a record of any kind, you will not go to prison. However, you will be placed on house arrest for a term of four months with five years' probation."

I closed my eyes with a sigh. Oh, thank God they're not sending me to prison. House arrest? What does that even mean? I can't go anywhere? What about work? Getting Angelica to school? Doctor appointments?

My state job ended abruptly when I asked if they would work around the conditions of my house arrest. With a felony conviction on my record, my only choice was to find something outside of my normal line of work. Starbucks seemed like a great place to work. I mustered up all the bravery I could while I observed the baristas brewing up special holiday drinks. The aroma of freshly ground coffee beans ignited my senses. The energy of the holiday frenzy boosted my metabolism.

I peeked around the end of the espresso bar to get a closer look at the lineup of hot and cold drink cups. The barista artfully steamed a pitcher of milk. I said, "That looks like fun. I'm here for an interview."

A woman surprised me from behind. "Are you, Cherie?"

When I turned, I saw a woman with a big smile and short, wavy platinum-blond hair. She gestured to a small table in the corner of the store. "Let's grab a seat away from the bar." She held out her hand. "My name is Kat. I'm the store manager."

I tried to maintain my composure. "Nice to meet you, Kat."

She cleared her throat. "So, Cherie, you stated on your application you have a felony conviction. You want to talk about that for a minute?"

Shame tried to take me out for a second, but I held my head high. "Uh, yeah. I suppose we better get that out of the way. It's pretty humbling." I pointed to the device around my ankle. I whispered, "I am on house arrest right now. This is my only offense. I'm trying not to lose custody of my daughter, and I had to give up a great job with the state."

Kat wore a look of surprise. "Wow, Cherie, I must say, I have a ton of respect for you. I'm a retired deputy sheriff, and I have seen and heard just about everything."

I pulled my head back in disbelief. "You're a retired cop?"

"Yes, and for you to come in here wearing that thing on your ankle … Well, let me put it this way…" She straightened her paperwork on the small bistro table, speaking in an encouraging tone. "You could have made up some story. But you didn't. You're owning your stuff. I'm offering you the job." Kat stood, collecting her latte cup and paperwork. "This is your second chance, Cherie. Keep doing the right thing. Are you with me?" she asked with a welcoming outstretched hand.

I wanted to hug the woman, but I shook her hand and thanked her for taking a chance on me.

The next four months were hell with Todd's antagonizing antics and efforts to sabotage my parenting time. I struggled to keep going and not give up on fighting for my daughter. He wanted me to blow it, which I did when I smashed his car window with a backpack. In my defense, he shouldn't have tried to run me over with the car—an incident our daughter witnessed.

I could barely make my share of the rent. I bartered away most of my belongings. One of the club members helped when issues came up with my car. Another brother helped with finances as long as I met his needs in return.

When my house arrest ended four months later, Lefty offered to let me live at his place rent-free. He moved into a travel trailer as caretaker of four hundred acres tucked in the foothills. In the spring, the ranch transformed into a serene paradise, with the hills radiating every shade of green. The road into the property crossed a levy. When the runoff from the snow melt in the Sierra Nevada Mountains made its way into the valley, the ponds transformed into a playground for the cats to jump across as they hunted frogs, polliwogs, and other goodies along the bank.

Kat, my manager at Starbucks, helped me transfer to another Starbucks store closer to Lefty's place which was thirty minutes away. My focus returned to preparing for my next family court hearing. The hearings became more frequent. Without the means to hire a family law attorney, I had no legal representation. I spent hours in the law library each week, researching forms and legal procedures. Regardless of the false accusations, I never gave up fighting for my daughter. I delved into parental alienation research and gained insight into effectively handling emergency ex parte orders.

I jumped through hoops to keep up with our parenting schedule. Todd did all he could to make it nearly impossible for me, either by sabotaging my daycare arrangements or not helping transport Angelica when I needed help. Now that I had a felony on my record and was on probation, he used that to his advantage, embellishing the truth about me in the courtroom.

He and his lawyer were experts at that, as if the facts were not bad enough. They made me out to be a homeless transient and stirred up hatred in my daughter's heart toward me. I refused to give up on her. And I certainly wasn't about to let her dad swoop her away, never seeing her again.

Maintaining a full-time work schedule helped my case. An added bonus came when my manager promoted me to shift supervisor. Earning more allowed me to pay my restitution through payroll deduction. I loved my regular customers.

One guy came in every morning when I opened the store at five o'clock. He owned a well-drilling business and rode with a local motorcycle club. His loyalties to the outlaw life and close ties to the mob drew me in. I found it difficult to resist the chemistry between us. My coworker helped me see what a bad choice I was about to make.

One of my other customers, Linda, worked across the street. She and I forged a deep bond through countless conversations at the counter, where she poured out the pain of her heart-wrenching divorce. She was a total knockout—tall, thin, brunette, and always dressed to the nines. I loved her soft-spoken demeanor all wrapped in her soft, white faux-fur coat. One morning when she mentioned joining a singles group at her church, I wanted to know more. Linda warmed her feminine manicured hands on her coffee cup. "Oh, it's a church in Folsom. Lakeside Church. You ought to check it out. I help at the Java counter. You can help me serve coffee. Kind of a perfect fit," she giggled.

That following Sunday, my new Christian friend took me to church with her. Lakeside Church sat on a hill. I liked their sign: A

Place to Begin. A Place to Belong. Families filled the lobby. People hugged each other. Within the first few minutes, a half dozen of my customers from Starbucks recognized me. Wow, it's like I returned home after a long time away. I finally found a home church. I wondered if God sent me there.

Lefty insisted on taking me to church rather than me going alone. He suspected I had met someone. His paranoia and jealousy over men and my new friends drove me crazy. I knew about his cheating as well. We fed each other's fears and insecurities. But there seemed to be a bond between us we simply could not let go of. I should have run the moment I uncovered his identity as a poser, but I could not fathom living alone again.

His ability to morph into a different persona frightened me. My daughter saw right through him and never trusted him. I was just as gullible as the judge or Social Security officer he fooled again and again. He knew how to manipulate my mind and my heart. I knew it and still could not break free.

One evening, I came home to find a pair of women's sandals by the back door. I saw red and destroyed precious mementos, dishes, and whatever else within my reach. When I flipped over his father's dining table, Lefty lunged at me and grabbed me by my neck. He about squeezed my airway closed tight with both hands.

Somehow, I managed to warn him, "If you hurt me, they will know, and you'll die." Given his state of mind, I was petrified, imagining him tossing me into the pit of slithering rattlesnakes beneath the back deck.

The next day, I fled to the safety of my church. But I still could not help but feel like an outcast. The few bikers I met at this church loved to ride Harleys, but they were not true bikers.

Lefty showed up early on a Sunday morning before church services and asked if he could vacuum the sanctuary.

One of the pastors asked, "So who is that character, Cherie?" He knew. I knew he did. It was as if he was seriously wondering how on earth I ended up with him, and whether I was in danger. I knew the answer. I'd witnessed his effortless ability to take on the identity of his best friend and how he'd prepared for weeks to transform his image into a destitute, unstable homeless man, all for government benefits.

I discovered just how much danger I was in when he confided that the FBI called him in for questioning in the East Area Rapist case. Lefty claimed the feds let him go without actually recognizing him as a suspect. Either way, the fact that he fit the profile caused underlying fear. Even so, I stayed. I would not allow him to keep me from going to work and spending time with my friends at the store. I headed straight to the church after work and volunteered my time working in the bookstore, which connected me with even more of my Starbucks customers.

The bookstore job was like heaven on earth. But then I began taking books home without paying for them. Sometimes I would return them, but other times I wouldn't. I prayed, Please, Lord, help me! I don't know why but I can't stop.

Angelica didn't want to be around Lefty and did not care for our living conditions. The small twenty-two-foot travel trailer only had one small bedroom, so she slept on the couch-bed. The court made it clear some changes needed to take place. After taking on a second job at a nearby Italian restaurant, I moved us into our own apartment. Since I could only afford a one-bedroom apartment, I slept on the couch when Angelica was home with me. She appreciated living closer to her school and her dad.

One morning, Linda came in for her regular white mocha and invited me to a Mary Kay tea party. I only agreed to go because she begged me. Linda introduced me to the lovely hostess and the other ladies, who were all close to my mother's age or older. I took my seat at the meticulously decorated dining table. We played games to win Scrabble pieces. Whoever ended up with the most Scrabble pieces won Mary Kay products.

I don't know how, but I answered the Mary Kay questions correctly and quickly built up my collection of tiles.

JAI …

A lump formed in my throat. Please don't let the next one be an L.

I drew the next tile.

L. Oh my God.

JAIL?

I hid my tiles and didn't say a word.

Chapter 17

Within forty-eight hours, two police officers came to my door in the middle of the night. They took me into custody for violation of probation. This made no sense to me. How could this happen while walking a straight line, following all the rules? I'm supposed to pick up Angelica from school tomorrow. What about my job? I haven't done anything wrong, God!

The female officer at the Sacramento County jail strip-searched me, grabbing at my chest and between my legs. She's counting on me to make a wrong move. I see it in her face. I stood there, eyes straight ahead, and did not react. Filled with humiliation and anger, I struggled to control myself from hitting her.

There were frequent news reports about the corruption in this place. I never imagined I'd experience it firsthand. My personal belongings were put into a brown paper bag and taken away in exchange for an orange jumpsuit, jailhouse underclothes, and tennis shoes. For the next several hours, I sat on the cold concrete floor of a cage. Women chattered, declaring their innocence. The cage, constructed of thick black steel bars, told otherwise.

I finally made it to a concrete cell the next afternoon. Exhausted, I lay back on the bottom bunk. I noticed a chilling message carved into the bottom of the top bunk: Welcome to Hell. I covered my face with both hands. I need to call Angelica. I need to call my mother. Oh, dear God, what is happening?

"Lights out, ladies!" the guard commanded over the PA system. The circular building reverberated with the piercing voice. The lights never went dark completely. The guards would not have that.

Fortunately, I landed in the lowest security block for women. Initially, all female inmates landed here, also referred to as the sorting floor. Depending on the severity of their crimes, some landed on the upper floors or transferred out to another facility altogether.

Relief flooded my mind as the locks disengaged the cell door the next morning at ten o'clock. I hurried to the pay phone and called my mother. Devastated and afraid for my life, she cried, "Why didn't you tell me? I would have helped you." Her tears stung. I held mine back. I could not allow the other women to see me break down. I tried to keep my voice to a whisper, but the large concrete dome with multiple floors echoed the voices of the hundreds of women in the block. "Mom, I'm not even sure how I got here. I need to talk to a public defender. They're saying I'll be here for thirty days. I can't stay here thirty days. I'll lose my job and my apartment. I could lose Angelica."

Through tears of agony only a loving mother could cry for her child, she asked how she could help. "I'm so sorry you're going through this."

I closed my eyes. In my calmest and lowest voice, I said, "Mom, I need you to come here. Please. Can you come tomorrow?" I could not say too much on the phone. "And I need you to call Todd. You need to tell him what's happened, and that I'll be in touch."

"Of course, sweetie. Stay strong. We'll be there tomorrow morning."

I gripped the pay phone with hesitation. Oh, how Todd's gonna love getting a collect call from me. Oh, how he wanted to see me destroyed … No answer. Great.

The guards brought two women, one by one, into my cell within the first seventy-two hours. Both mentioned charges of serious drug-related crimes. My first roomie could not sit still. She paced the floor and jumped up on and down off her bunk, anxious to get released. Confinement seemed to send her in a tizzy. She stood staring out the narrow window of the cell door, biting her nails. "So whatchu in for?" She never broke her gaze.

I found it odd that inmates exchanged crimes before exchanging names. At least she wanted to break the ice, so I took the bait. "Violation of probation. Still not sure what that means exactly. How about you?"

She leaned against the cell door. Her lips tightened and her voice agitated, she answered, "Possession. Caught me with methamphetamine. Damn pigs. I hate 'em." Taking a deep breath, she smiled and sighed. "That's okay though. I'll be out today."

I straightened my blankets and turned to face the wall. "Wish I could say that. They're telling me I'll be here for thirty days." My thoughts scattered. I may actually lose my job. My daughter. What am I doing here, Lord? Please keep me in this cell unless it's time for me to go home. Please, Jesus.

The echoes of cell doors opening and closing filled the block. Women rushed to take showers before lockdown. Dinner left much to be desired. Alone in my cell again, I munched on the apple I saved from lunch. A woman's screams echoed from across the block. The other inmates yelled at her to shut up.

"She can't hear you! She's deaf!" one woman yelled.

I read in the welcome booklet that you could order a Bible from the jail chaplain, but it stated in fine print: It may take up to two weeks to fulfill your request.

Two weeks to get a Bible?

I guess God was listening, because the next day, the woman in the cell next to mine gave me her Bible when she left. I held it close to my chest. Oh, thank you, Jesus. You are here, Lord. Help me get to the phone today. I need to take care of so many things.

Later, I made contact with my manager at Starbucks. He committed to holding my job for three more days. I expressed my thanks to him with profound gratitude. My next task was to find someone to break into my apartment to check on my cat. Linda refused to take my calls. Some friend. After I went with her to that stupid Mary Kay party.

I finally contacted a guy from church. When Linda introduced us, he told me his friends called him Special Ed because his name is Ed, and … he's special. What a character. Special Ed tried to make excuses for Linda bailing on me. She lived a sheltered life and never met anyone in trouble with the law. He said it freaked her out since she invited me into her house. Special Ed assured me I did not have to worry about my kitty. He gave me another phone number where he could receive my collect calls. Another friend of his from church would also help me out with whatever they could. Special Ed had my back. I thanked God for sending help.

Having the cell to myself gave me quiet time to fill out a request form to see a public defender. After that, I worked on a poem for my angel babe. My little wing. Reading from the Psalms kept me from overthinking about this place. Angel must be so disappointed in me. At nine years old, my daughter understood more than the average young girl. My only form of contact with her so far was writing letters filled with words of love and encouragement. I couldn't be sure if she saw them or not.

I curled up beneath the thin, wool blanket with the Bible tucked beneath my arm. I'd survive this hellhole. The words written in the book protected my mind from horrific attacks of despair and hopelessness. They would counteract the evil, often demonic messages carved into the walls. I decided to lay at the opposite end of the bunk, so I didn't need to see the "welcome" sign on the bed above. The last thing I needed to read upon waking or before falling asleep was "Welcome to Hell."

The moment I managed to relax and find solace in the warmth of the blanket, the unsettling sound of scuffling outside the cell door disturbed my rest. I moaned and raised my head from beneath the covers. The clanging of the disengaging cell door echoed through the jail when the night guard delivered my third cell mate. The sound of the unlocking door offered a glimpse of freedom. I quickly chased away my thoughts of escape.

The exhausted woman struggled with the weight of the door while carrying her bundled bedding under one arm and a pillow and Ziploc bag of personal hygiene items in the other. I made brief eye contact with her as she reached for the top bunk. Without a sound, I transformed my bath towel into a makeshift curtain, shielding myself from the blinding light that seeped through the small six by six-inch window on the solid steel cell door .

The guard announced on the speaker, "Lights out, ladies!"

I visualized Angelica's pure, innocent face. I wanted so badly to wrap my arms around her and tell her everything would be all right. I'm so sorry I'm not there with you, bellissima Principessa. I cried myself to sleep.

Right on cue, two hours after falling asleep, the guard announced, "Wake up, ladies!" Cell count took place several times a day. During the night shift, it usually occurred a couple hours after lights out. Other nights, for some reason, the guard would make the rounds every two hours. Regardless, a good night's sleep was not possible in the Sacramento County Jail. One advantage of cell count happening at night was that the guards didn't insist on the women getting fully dressed or standing at attention before the cell door window. Perhaps their motive at night was to catch a glimpse of us partially dressed. Most of the female guards were obvious about their sexual preference for women.

Barely awake, I slowly sat up on the edge of my bunk. I made sure the night guard could see my ID bracelet through the window. The guard's steps echoed around the top floor of the block, intensifying the closer he got to our cell. He walked past our door with a quick nod of approval. A blessing, no doubt, since all I wanted was a peaceful night's rest. That pour soul screaming from across the block certainly didn't help matters.

My cellie found it difficult to sleep too. Boldly, she said, "I'm Jessie…Jessie Santos. What's your name?" She pulled the towel aside from my makeshift cabana.

Startled, I propped myself up on one elbow. Jessie stood at the side of my bunk, undernourished and street weary. She looked Portuguese, with a drug-scarred complexion and dark, sunken eyes, telling of a hard life. Regardless, I could not help but admire her Southern European beauty resonating beneath her hardened shell. Shaking off my need for sleep, I appreciated her friendly nature. "I'm Cherie. Nice to meet you. They sure brought you in late. You must be wiped out."

Jessie leaped up to the top bunk like a small child would. She released a heavy sigh while straightening her bedding. "Yeah, I can always count on a good night's sleep when I'm in though. What are you in for? Man, you hear that girl screamin'?"

Bewildered, I said, "I don't know who it is, but she screams day and night." Shuffling my pillow, I shared about my confusion over being hauled in here for nothing. "It sounds like you're in here often." I yawned.

Jessie described the night of her arrest when she messed up one of her clients. While lifting the guy's wallet from his pants, he allegedly grabbed Jessie by her locks of hair. Breaking a beer bottle over his face led her here with charges of assault and prostitution. It was no surprise to see Jessie so relaxed. This wasn't her first rodeo. Her ownership of her crimes, casual. The consequences did not seem to matter. This was just one more stop among many for Jessie.

I imagined she must find more rest here than out on the streets. I sensed that getting locked up now and again was her way of surviving. This wasn't Jessie's hell. A jail cell provided safe haven.

Jessie boasted, "They'll be sendin' me away, probably the next day or so. Maybe back to Yolo. That place is like a retreat, with vending machines, great food, and you get more time outside too. Nothing like here."

In a pause of quiet stillness between us, I pondered in disbelief how a person could associate incarceration with a retreat. But then, my grandmother used to tell my mom she was away at the country club when the police hauled her in for driving drunk. Yawning, I randomly flipped through the thin pages of my Bible.

Jessie's curiosity broke our brief moment of silence. "What are ya readin'?

I explained I like to read the Bible before falling asleep, since it keeps my mind from playing games on me. She surprised me when she asked if I could read it out loud. I propped up the Bible on my pillow and read from Ephesians. I browsed the pages and read select nuggets from chapter four. "Stop telling lies. Don't let anger control you. Anger gives a foothold to the devil. Quit stealing. Work hard and give to those in need. Don't use foul or abusive language. And do not bring sorrow to God's Holy Spirit by the way you live. Get rid of all bitterness and rage … Instead, be kind to each other, tenderhearted, forgiving one another, just as God through Christ has forgiven you."

I chuckled at the irony. "Wow, seems a bit fitting. That's the way God rolls."

Jessie said softly, "You know, when I walked into this cell, it felt different, like a glow of light."

We called it a night with the hope for a restful sleep.

Sadness fell upon me when cries crept into my slumber. I stirred beneath the blanket, realizing the cries were not a dream. Not mine, anyway. It only took another second to clear my drowsiness. I tucked the Bible between the mattress and cell wall.

More whimpers, gasps, and short breaths came from the top bunk. I began to pray. Dear God, please send an angel to comfort Jessie's dreams. Remove her pain and fill her dreams with your love. Bring her peace. Amen. Jessie's pleas continued for several minutes, eventually calming to whimpers once more. After a short pause, her whimpers turned to sobbing. Her nightmare startled her awake.

Neither one of us slept much that night. I lay there wide awake when the five o'clock wakeup sounded. My stomach churned and growled. I kept my eyes forward and did not say a word when I picked up my breakfast tray of grayish-brown hot cereal, a small carton of milk, a fresh orange, and a small bran muffin. I put the orange aside for later and ate everything else. I tried to lay back down to grab another hour of sleep before they called for us to place our trays outside the cell door.

Jessie leaned down over the edge of her bunk. "Hey, I liked what you read last night. Can we read more later?"

I moved my makeshift curtain aside, and her dark curls dangled from her bunk. "Sure, we can do that."

"I liked that part about anger and forgiveness."

"You too, huh?"

Jessie sat up on the edge of her bunk with her legs hanging down. "Yeah, I've tried forgiving my family. It's not easy. Especially now that they know the truth about my cousin."

Over the next couple hours, she poured her heart out to me, a total stranger. She described herself as a problem child. Her mother sent her away to live with her aunt and uncle in the Oak Park area of south Sacramento when she was ten years old. Jessie's younger brother and six-month-old baby sister were about all her mother could handle.

Her older cousin invited her to explore the fort he and a friend built in a nearby alley. It was within that very place where Jessie's innocence was stolen. She endured repeated attacks by her cousin and his buddies. Jessie's words conveyed how her mother sent her to live with her relatives as a form of punishment. She went on to describe the pain of keeping her secret until she finally found the courage to say something to her uncle.

When she did, her uncle grabbed hold of her and commanded that she never tell those lies again. Her uncle, assigned to protect her, proceeded to beat her. Jessie ran away that night into Oak Park.

She described how fear and confusion held her captive. A man soon picked her up and used her for sex.

This became Jessie's life. Even after meeting a good man, who she married and birthed four children, she continued to chase her demons into the streets of Oak Park. She finally told her husband and children they were better off without her.

My heart ached for Jessie. Reminders of my sister pained me. I thanked God for protecting me from similar dangers. Things could have been so much worse. When I asked her if she ever talked to her children, she said she called to check in now and then. It sounded like their father provided a safe and loving home. What must they think of her? What must my angel babe think of me?

Jessie went on to tell me her cousin served time in prison on rape charges. She sighed heavily. "Bad things happen to people like him in prison. Karma will get him."

"Knowing how God works, your cousin may experience a different kind of justice."

"Hey, you figure my uncle finally believes me?"

"The question is, how could he not believe you? I imagine he's carried some guilt all these years."

"Yeah, I know it wasn't his fault."

Jessie changed the subject. "Hey, I noticed you writing." The pitch of her voice lowered. "Would you write a letter to my aunt and uncle for me? I ... I think I need to tell them ... it's not their fault and I forgive them. I'm wondering if they believe me now."

While Jessie shared from her heart, I helped her articulate the words and pen them onto the jail-issued note paper. I realized that my purpose for being in this dreadful place was for a positive outcome, according to God.

The next morning, Jessie mailed the envelope and transferred to another facility. Having the cell to myself for the next couple of days gave me time to think and pray. I got word about my appointment with the public defender and prepared to beg and plead my way out of there.

Two days later, she and I sat on either side of a glass window. A dark-haired woman wearing a light blue button-down shirt peered through her reading glasses and examined my file. I kept my hands folded on the cold stainless-steel counter. She looked me straight in the eyes and with a compassionate tone. "Cherie, you don't belong in here. I'll get you out, but you have to give me a couple days. It's not possible to make this happen any faster than that." The lady leaned close to the speaker in the glass window. "Are you okay?"

A wave of relief fell over me. Nearly crying, I said, "Yes, God has my back. Two guards tore apart my cell for no reason. They took everything but my writing. Please … get me to my daughter."

I couldn't sleep at all that night. Reflecting on the days with Jessie brought clarity. My poor self-esteem could not comprehend how God could use me for His purpose in Jessie's life after failing Him so. I sensed God calling me to forgive. I slept better that night knowing I'd be sorted out of jail in a matter of days.

Though I did not belong in here, God made some good come from it.

Chapter 18

Stepping out of the Sacramento County Jail after two grueling weeks, I found myself thrust into a new, unfamiliar reality. My probation officer sat across from the desk, reviewing my file. With every ounce of restraint in me, I maintained my composure. Though, I was certain my body language revealed my contention for her. The woman folded her hands, searching for her words before making eye contact. "I wouldn't blame you if you hated me right now." She explained how the revenue accounting office misappropriated the money withheld from my payroll. Instead of applying it to my outstanding restitution, they'd applied it to old traffic tickets.

I felt my face flush red and my heart pound faster. A mistake? Calm down, Cherie. Exploding right here will not help the situation. My entire life is in this woman's control. Deep breath. Forgive.

In the court's eyes, I'd failed to comply with the terms of my probation. I should have sued all of them, but now I'd clean up the wreckage and move forward. My boss could not hold my job which resulted in giving up my apartment.

Returning to Lefty's was my only option. Fear, shame, and pain continued to pour from my heart through poetry and journaling my life story. The ponds on Lefty's ranch became a place to purge and heal. My friends at my new church offered tremendous support while I found my footing all over again.

When the opportunity to volunteer in the church bookstore came up, I jumped at it. I loved books. Serving there held me accountable and gave me a reason to be there every day.

One of the pastors encouraged me to get counseling. I recognized the importance of finding someone who held safe, if not similar, spiritual beliefs. The last thing I wanted was another bad experience.

In my research, I learned some psychologists followed the belief that survivors of childhood sexual abuse bore some responsibility for their perpetrator's sexual psychosis. Browsing the internet, I discovered a myriad of support groups including a local women's shelter, none of which were faith-based. That concerned me. My pastor thought I should check them out, chew on the meat, and spit out the bones.

His advice helped me show up at The Center for Violence-Free Relationships with a healthier mindset. Their office sat tucked in the corner suite of an old office complex up in the mountains. An "Open" sign hung from the paned window of the weathered wooden door. The lobby furniture, just as weathered, included two chairs and a loveseat, all dating back to the 1960s. A large wicker basket sat on a table with a note card that read: "Donations for Women's Center."

The intake counselor asked me to complete a questionnaire to help her determine my needs. I sat in the brown, weathered office chair with a clipboard full of forms. Here we go. I skimmed the list of behavioral characteristics to which I could relate.

Nightmares. Distorted body image. Internal scarring. Oh yeah, that too. That pig. Aversion to dentists. Compulsive behaviors. Cutting. Yeah, I suppose tattoos qualify. Anxiety. Need to be perfect or perfectly bad. Yep, that's me. Suicidal thoughts. At times. Depression.

This list is making me depressed. Anger. Inability to trust. Rage when trust is broken. They hit that one on the head. High risk taking. Check. Control issues. Yep. Sexual confusion. Oh no, now I have to talk about this? Sexual issues. Wow, they have a whole paragraph for that one. Stealing. Hypervigilance regarding child abuse. I sat there for a couple minutes, staring out the office window. I might as well check off every one of them. I'm an absolute mess.

Sherrie, my intake counselor, checked out my assessment and asked if I was up for discussing the next step. Pulling myself from the swamp of self-pity, I asked, "Can you tell me about the support group for women survivors? I'm interested in participating in that group."

I noticed a collage of written testimonies framed on the wall of Sherrie's office. One story in particular resonated with me. This woman charged straight through her storm, determined she'd end up stronger on the other side. Her bravery left me standing in awe. I need to do this. My baby girl deserves a better life and a healthy mother who she can count on. The demons of my past were like relentless hounds, always at my heels, and I couldn't let them chase me any longer. All the while, the need to forgive my family continued to impress upon my heart. Maybe I could eventually forgive myself.

Years before, I'd come upon a church in which the pastor's teaching on forgiveness pierced my heart. It freed me from wanting to kill my brother-in-law. I was still trying to wrap my mind around if God expected me to forgive everyone in one fell swoop.

At the age of forty-one, I realized the importance of re-establishing a relationship with my father. Angelica, now ten years old, had missed out on a relationship with her only grandfather. I wanted to change that. Two years had passed since I last saw my father. I imagined it hurt him knowing I lived only two hours away. But I figured it goes both ways. It was only right to reconnect with his birthday and Father's Day coming up.

To my surprise, when I called, Rose explained my father left for Romania on a mission trip with their pastor. He'd be gone for a couple of weeks. She described how Dad had begun attending services with her at their small Baptist church. "God finally got a hold of your dad. He's not the same man anymore. He sat in the back of that church, yelling out questions to the preacher, holding him accountable whenever something didn't sound right. Now, he can't stop singing for the Lord. He's spending more time with the kids, and everyone's happier."

After I picked my jaw up from the floor, happiness welled up in me for my father. I wiped the tears from my eyes. "Wow, that's incredible. If you talk to him, tell him I called to wish him a Happy Birthday and Happy Father's Day, okay? Tears of admiration and pride filled my eyes. "And please tell Dad I love him."

In a sweet tone, Rose said, "Why don't you call back in a couple of weeks. You can tell him. And I'm sure he'll tell you all about his trip."

I detected a subtle tremor in her voice, or perhaps it was the pounding of my own heart, urging me to reconcile with my father. God's ability to change my dad's heart was nothing short of a miracle. What a radical transformation, from a warrior outlaw biker to a warrior for Christ.

Could we finally have a real relationship? I wanted that so badly. His step-grandchildren knew him as their father. My heart ached for a piece of my father I never knew as a child. Why do they get that when I never did? It took time to understand they simply got the best years of his life.

Our next conversation filled my heart with joy and anticipation. I looked forward to getting to know my father all over again. Eager to hear about his adventure, I asked, "Tell me about your trip. I can't even believe I didn't know you were going to Romania. You? A missionary?" I laughed.

He chuckled a little. "You know, I thought I grew up poor." He paused. "We have no idea what poor is here. We don't have a clue. These poor kids are living in the dirt. No clean water. They wait in line for potatoes. They're lucky if they get a bath, and it's with buckets of cold water. I did my small part to help build a place where they have a bed to sleep in and a bathroom." He laughed and told me how much they loved the hard candies he brought for them and that he promised to send more.

Laughing at his ways with children through the tears of a proud daughter, I told him about everything going on with Todd in court. Todd incessantly called my father to get him to pick sides. One day, my dad put his foot down and told him, "I don't know what you think you're doing, but this is my daughter we're talking about. I will not side with you on this. So, I suggest you don't call me again." Todd got the message and that was the last time he contacted my father.

Learning how my father stood up for me reminded me of the story my mom told me about my father scooping her away to keep my grandmother from forcing her to abort me. Another story Mom shared was how my father defended her honor by decking his commanding officer while stationed at Fort Benning. The fiasco led to an honorable discharge from the U.S. Army and avoided deployment to Vietnam where his entire unit perished.

And now he honored me. My heart filled with deep love for my father during our call. I recalled his rough upbringing, without a father to guide him. Pain and unforgiveness washed away. I couldn't wait to see him again. Unfortunately, I couldn't leave Sacramento County without approval from my probation officer. They only granted the green light for urgent matters. No overnight trips allowed. My dad understood.

Excited to share my news with my intake counselor, I showed up early. I checked out a nearby bookstore to kill some time. Inspired to finally write about my crazy life, I searched the shelves for a book about motorcycle clubs. When I located a book of interest on the bottom of a large bookshelf, a book directly above it caught my attention. Secret Survivors. Incest. I flipped open the hard cover and squealed, "What?" I was so shocked that I believe I yelled.

The exact intake questionnaire I completed for my counselor was part of the inside binding of the front cover. Apparently, the clinical questionnaire was based on The Incest Survivors' Aftereffects Check-list contained in this book. In that moment, I made a commitment to the program. I believed God placed the book in front of me to show me I was right where He wanted me.

Days later, another dream etched itself into my memory. This time, I rode on a local city bus, seated directly across from the bus driver. The driver turned his head in my direction. His face glowed, absent of facial details. His glow exuded peace when he said, "What are you doing on this bus? You must get off this guilt trip to experience the blessings I have for you."

I could not hold back the wonder of how God showed up in my dreams. My eyes opened. I reached for my phone. 3:00 a.m. I lay there, questioning the meaning. Guilt trip? The same blank, glowing face in the "Tell them—Romans 10" dream. Another message from God?

The dreams kept coming, so I kept my journal next to the bed. I wrote more and more poems and about bits and pieces of my crazy life. I quickly wrote down every detail of the dream, naming this one 'The Guilt Trip.'

A number of things made me feel guilty. Failing my little girl, for one. My marriage. The marriages I'd damaged. The lies, stealing, abandoning my friends … everything. As I went down my inventory list, it hit me. Unforgiveness. Self-rejection. I get it. I need to forgive myself. But how?

Our support group took a break for the holidays. My probation officer granted a pass to visit my father for Christmas. A surge of overwhelming joy and gratitude filled my soul. The week before Christmas, Angelica and I met Dad and Rose at their church. Their grandchildren joined the rest of the youth group to rehearse for their Christmas production. He and my stepmom now possessed legal guardianship of their grandchildren. God redeemed those years he'd walked away from Jami and me as little girls.

My father instructed the kids about the Christmas performance. I looked at Rose in amazement. "Dad's the youth leader?" Go figure. He always loved children and they always loved him. Naturally, the younger kiddos thought he was Santa throughout the year because of his full white beard. No more bikers. No more drugs. A new man.

He shared a song with me by Third Day, a Christian rock group. God put their song, Sing a Song, on his heart, and he wanted to sing it. The night of the Christmas play, he walked in wearing his navy-blue suit and a Christmas tie with a cross on it. It felt good to feel his big bear hug around me. Nothing could remove my smile. I proudly stood beside him for a family picture. My daddy loves Jesus.

Those couple of days with my father at Christmas flew by. Returning to Lefty's, I found myself alone on New Year's Eve. Seated on the couch in Lefty's cramped travel trailer, I flipped through my journal to the first blank page. December 31, 2005. Pulling my soft, fluffy throw over my legs, I noticed my last entry. August. That's a month I'd like to erase. I'd bounced back and forth from the ranch to an apartment and returning to the ranch again felt wrong.

The court knew it wasn't good either and ordered me not to have Angel around Lefty or at this place. Todd punished me by having the court suspend my parenting time on last Mother's Day because of my defiance. I couldn't come up with any other options—or so I believed.

I hesitated as I considered a resolution for the new year. I'm not making any resolutions this year. I never keep them, anyway. Look at me now. Nothing like ten years ago. We were happy with all of our friends. My life was good. Great job. Happy family. I miss my life. I miss my friends.

Memories of my three dearest, most loyal friends were heavy on my heart. Monica, John, and Cindy seemed to have completely vanished from my life. How could I let that happen? Did they even think about me anymore? I couldn't handle telling them about everything that happened after my divorce or the events leading up to it. How did I end up here? I'd been so on fire for the Lord.

My failures mounted in my mind, reliving the dreadful, revisiting torment. In the most horrific places of my life, my mind locked my past in a hidden chamber. If only the flashbacks would somehow die. Moans and cries deep from a dungeon-like prison rose, as though I could feel Satan's fury, knowing he would no longer keep me captive, How dare you forsake me?

Memories left unattended and forgotten returned with fury, demanding a place in my life. Their manifestations jolted my psyche. When life appeared good, these ghosts from the past wreaked havoc in my subconscious. I did not understand how I ended up believing goodness was not welcome. It seemed foreign to my soul.

Evil intended to destroy any form of goodness. The devil convinced me I did not deserve a good life. How dare I crash the party as an impostor? Grasping at the back of my head with my hands, I did all I could to silence the shame and guilt. Fear and condemnation fought me at every attempt.

I buried my face in the blanket and screamed, "How did I get so far away from you, Lord? This is not who I am!"

I've never left you.

Tears faded. The words were nearly audible. I looked around the cramped travel trailer. "What? God?" I closed my eyes, Calm, then sorrow fell over me.

Lord, I'm so sorry. I don't know what to do. I'm about to lose my little girl, God! I've already lost her heart and her love. I can't lose her! She's yours, God! Can she ever forgive me? I dedicated her to you … and I blew it. I promised. I'm so sorry. They're spewing so many lies. Please don't let them take my baby away. I obviously don't know what it looks like to have a relationship with you, I prayed. You have to show me. I promise that nobody will ever come before you again. I don't know what happened to my life! God, forgive me. Help bring John and Monica and Cindy back into my life. You know how much they mean to me. Show me the way out of this wilderness! I need to know what is of you and what isn't, Lord. I'm praying for wisdom to know the difference. I'm so tired of falling prey to deception.

The sincere plea from my anguished heart ignited a dormant fire within me, propelling me forward. I don't know any other way to explain it, but God planted a desire in my heart and mind to read my Bible. All my answers were right there, and I could not put it down.

My pocket Bible went everywhere with me. I read and read and read. The sheer fascination of the truths I unraveled fueled my determination to find the next one. The Scripture given to me years ago when I first encountered God echoed in my memory. *For I know the plans I have for you, says the Lord. They are plans for good and not for evil, to give you a future and hope.* (Jeremiah 29:11 TLB).

I understood this passage to say God would never cause me harm. His plans are better than mine. Reading the verses surrounding this one put it into the proper context and gave me a better understanding of the circumstances in my life. The intention of Jeremiah 29:11 wasn't to eradicate my suffering, but to assist me in navigating it and instill hope for the future God intended for me.

I saw this truth come to life within weeks, in a dream of my father. I sat in a white room at a white table with my former mother-in-law. She crafted Easter gifts for her grandchildren. My brother sat across from me. The atmosphere was filled with a profound sense of grief and sorrow. We both stood and held each other, as if to comfort. Our father stood in the corner of the room, leaning back with his arms crossed over the chest of his white gown. He observed us, though we did not see him.

The dream jarred me awake. I nudged Lefty. "Wake up. I dreamed about my dad." An urgency came over me. Wow. That seemed so real. "I need to call him. Where's my phone?" Sliding across the bed to get up, I picked it up. Missed call? Oh yeah, I turned off the ringer. There's a message … my stepmom? What on earth?

I listened to the voice mail and heard Rose's voice, weak and shaking. "Cherie, call me as soon as you get this."

The timestamp on her message read 3:00 a.m., four hours ago. Overcome with dread, I set the phone down and turned to Lefty. A knowing pressed on my heart. "My dad's gone." Almost afraid to call, I sat and prayed first.

When I finally called, Rose sobbed on the other end of the line. She did her best to explain what happened. They had set out in the early morning hours for a road trip from Corning, California, to Washington state to pick up a car and visit my aunt Betty, dad's older sister. Dad, Rose, and their two grandchildren loaded up in the van with a car trailer in tow. They printed out the lyrics to Dad's favorite song, "Spirit in the Sky."

They would practice singing it together while on the road. Dad longed to sing it in church. On their way to the highway, Dad drove through the neighborhood on the dark country road when he glanced in his rearview mirror. Upon seeing a truck pull up to their house, he decided to swing by again and see what was going on.

Rose described how the van veered off the road, crashing through the neighbor's fence into their plowed field. At first Rose thought my dad might have dozed off. She gently shook him, but his lifeless body was unresponsive. Fortunately, Rose thought to shut off the ignition and bring the van to a safe stop.

I couldn't fathom all they'd endured that night. Rose and the children walked back to the house, only to find that the small orange pickup my dad saw parked in front of the house had disappeared. There was a profound knowing in my heart that God sent His angels to keep my father from reaching the highway. Dad's heart gave out in an instant. Just like Jami, He orchestrated the perfect timing of my father's home-going and protected the rest of the family.

He gave my father a vision of an orange truck, causing him to turn back. Dad may have also sensed a tightening in his chest, and created the story, not to cause panic, but to get his family back to the house.

Either way, God intervened.

Chapter 19

A new music video, *Jesus Take the Wheel*, comforted me in my grief and brought peace. My writing took a different turn toward honoring my father, infusing it with deeper significance. Excavating the roots of my past gave shape to my life story. I took the time to enjoy sunrises and sunsets with Jesus by the pond. Each day, my encounters with Jesus led to further healing. My father's legacy would carry on in my book.

Angelica expressed her gratitude for taking her to visit her grandfather at Christmas. She valued the time to become better acquainted with him. I felt a sense of relief knowing that she would remember her grandpa for the wonderful person he was in his last days.

Our relationship improved too, except for her disapproval and anger over my ongoing relationship with Lefty. I knew I had to break away, but an indescribable pull kept me connected to him. My financial situation prevented me from securing a place for us. While recovering from a work-related surgery, I relied on a small monthly check from the disability office as my only income. I finally realized fear of the unknown kept me in bondage to this man.

Another surprise ex parte order came, stirring hatred in me. Why are they driven to take my only child from me? When is this going to stop, Lord? They're relentless liars!

I opened my Bible and researched verses about God's justice. One of the first verses I landed on was Matthew 10:26 (NIV): "So do not be afraid of them, for there is nothing concealed that will not be disclosed or hidden that will not be made known." Wow, that's it. He sure repeats "Don't be afraid" a lot through this chapter. I need to pray this in the courtroom.

When I began praying that Scripture over the lawyer, the judge, and even the bailiff, strange things began happening in the courthouse. My ex-husband's lawyer, who vowed to never let me see my daughter again, began making a fool of himself in the court clerk's office. One morning I responded to another emergency ex parte hearing. While waiting for my hearing, the clerk told me the lawyer did not file the necessary forms and that I could go home. The lawyer chased me down the hallway, yelling, "Stop! You better not go out that door!" Security reported him to the court, leading to a reprimand from the judge.

The following week, I wore my most conservative outfit and pulled my hair up to polish the look. Entering the courthouse always gave me anxiety, especially knowing my ex's attorney was out for blood. Today, an air of confidence strengthened me. Walking down the palatial hall with court files in hand, I prayed fervently. Reveal your truth to the judge, Lord. Show him what they're trying to do. Protect us, Jesus. Thank you for fighting for my baby girl. Amen.

I reflected on my failure to my vow to God concerning my precious daughter. I was terrible at keeping promises to anyone. Here we were, in our fifth painful year of this court battle. Our daughter endured much trauma through mediation, counselors, and fights between her father and me.

I took my seat at the table, swearing to tell the truth, the whole truth, and nothing but the truth, so help me, God. I organized my paperwork. Oh God, I pray justice over this courtroom and everyone in it. You are a God of justice. Thank you, God. Amen.

With a different judge on the bench, my thoughts became muddled, unsure of what to think. He announced Judge Nelson would no longer preside over our case and he would take over. The judge took a few minutes to scan our file. He looked at Todd's lawyer. In disbelief, he raised his voice. "I can't believe how long this case has been dragging on. I do not see anything proving this mother is unfit. All joint custody orders will remain as is. The mother shall not forfeit primary custody. This case is dismissed. Good luck to you both."

With a slam of his gavel, my fight ended. I sat there in awe of God. Holding my tears back, I thanked the judge. He nodded and placed our case file aside.

Folding my hands in front of my face, I closed my eyes. Thank you, God. Thank you for hearing my cries and for revealing the truth.

Articles I found later shed light on the corrupt nature of our original judge, ultimately leading to his removal from the bench. That hit me hard, but in a good way. God showed He was a God of justice, and His truth prevailed.

More than ever, I felt God nudging me to leave Lefty's ranch. The church asked me to increase my hours, another sign of God's pursuit. My spirit began to sense the difference between the peaceful, loving atmosphere at the church and the revolting heaviness at the ranch. Feeling out of place at church, I remained guarded. I didn't fit in, nor did I interact with many people there. Their genuine intentions became evident over time, and I learned to trust them.

One Sunday, I accepted an invitation to be baptized at the upcoming baptism celebration on the American River. I immediately called my mom and brother to share the excitement, and to extend an invitation to the celebration, scheduled for two weeks out. My mother couldn't see why baptism was necessary. Despite my attempts to explain, Mom held onto the belief that my Catholic baptism as an infant was satisfactory. Angelica couldn't make it because she was with her father that weekend. I counted on my brother and his family to celebrate with me.

Lefty parked close to the trail leading to the river. We set up our picnic spot on the grass, away from the other sixty or so churchgoers, most of who were there to be baptized. Their quick glances made me uneasy. Looking around, I realized I wasn't the only one with tattoos. I approached the pastor who I'd talked to about getting baptized. When he asked me to take the mic and share a little about my testimony, I knew I couldn't say no. He knew how to build bridges and I appreciated him breaking the ice for me.

After lunch, our group walked down the dirt path to the water, Three of our pastors lined up in the cool water. Despite moving into the beginning of summer, the American River was surprisingly cool as a result of the snow melt from the mountains. Standing in waist-deep, frigid water, each of the three pastors had a line of at least a dozen people in front of them. The joyous occasion took our attention away from the biting cold of the river.

I walked from the rocky beach into the water. Pastor Jim placed one hand on my forehead and the other on my shoulder. "Cherie, beloved child of God, I baptize you in the name of the Father, Son, and Holy Spirit." He lowered me backward into the water, fully submerging me into the river.

When he lifted me up, I felt a euphoric presence like I'd never felt. In that moment, all the noise of the world faded away into silence. My steps were light as I made my way to the gravelly beach. Clearing the water from my eyes, I saw my brother walking toward me, smiling and clapping with joy.

With each passing week, my uneasiness grew stronger whenever I returned home after volunteering at the church. A heaviness fell on my heart as soon as I drove up to the large livestock gate. Something around the ranch felt evil and disturbed my spirit. Lefty and I became more distant. He admitted to not knowing who I was anymore. I took that as a compliment and moved out.

Leaving Lefty enabled me to surround myself with people who encouraged my faith and healing. This changed my daughter's perception of me which gained her trust. The work God had to do in me continued into a season of forgiveness. Ironically, I learned from my brother that Van survived another violent attack. This latest incident left him in a vegetative state, under intensive care at a long-term care facility. I struggled to extend any form of compassion toward him. Serves him right. Forgive, Cherie. Forgive him. How am I going to do this? He deserves every bit of what he's getting. It's worse than death. He did this to himself.

But God had a way with placing things in my path. While waiting for my evening support group session to begin, I picked up a copy of a free weekly newspaper in front of the supermarket. The feature article detailed the case of a death row inmate who fired his lawyer for trying to save his life. Who did that?

The man, who brutally raped and murdered two women, was sentenced to death row at San Quentin. The lawyer read about the case in the newspaper and began digging into the prisoner's family tree. He uncovered a horrific history of alcoholism, physical and mental abuse, pedophilia, sexual molestation, and mental illness spanning three generations. The history included the violent beatings and molestation the man received at the hands of his own father, as well as near-constant abuse from his mother and stepfather.

A federal judge reversed the death sentence because the evidence of systematic abuse was so convincing. However, the state pressed on.

The prisoner told his lawyer, "You can present anything you want in court as long as I don't have to be there." He refused to testify on his own behalf and relive the unbearable pain and memories, even to spare his own life. Apparently, some secrets are so painful, they're worth taking to the grave. The vivid memory of the night when Roger's friends raped me without any struggle came rushing back.

The story brought me to tears. An innocent little boy, beaten, poisoned, and raped, turned into a pedophile, murderer, and monster. I'd spare his life too. Knowing how his past shaped him stopped me in my tracks. What caused my stepfather to do what he did to us? Why did my father leave? What were their demons? What about Mom? Her mom? Look at what I've done … and God forgives me.

Drug abuse is extremely damaging neurologically, and Van suffered a life-altering traumatic brain injury. The only reason I could feel compassion for Van was because of God's supernatural power. Though I grieve the trauma and destruction he caused in our family, I forgave him. This breakthrough catapulted me into a need for deeper understanding and built a resolve in me to continue doing the hard work to heal.

And the breakthroughs kept coming.

A pivotal moment came when I met Diane, a new friend from church, for coffee at Borders. We talked about my crazy family and my background. She seemed intrigued but not shocked. She suggested I write a book. I assured her Biker Blood was in the works.

After saying our goodbyes, I happened upon a display of a highly marketed Christian book, Become a Better You, by Joel Osteen. My gas-guzzling truck and the state of my pocketbook kept me from purchasing a copy. Instead, I returned to my comfy chair in the café to browse through this book. I skimmed the table of contents. Hmmm... The Power of Your Bloodline.

Regardless of my messy natural bloodline, we possess champion qualities. Really?

I have a biblical bloodline?

This compelled me to consider my own characteristics and strengths. But even then, I doubted my worth in light of the greatness in God's promises. The book's truths about the power of my spiritual and natural bloodline contradicted the internal lies I believed about myself.

Until ... I sensed the infusion of God's truth, the rebranding of my soul, right there in the café of Borders Books. I pulled out my journal to record the words so I would not forget them.

> *"When someone becomes a Christian, he becomes a*
> *brand-new person inside. He is not the same anymore. A*
> *new life has begun!" (2 Corinthians 5:17 TLB)*

> *"But you are a chosen people, a royal priesthood, a holy nation, God's*
> *special possession, that you may declare the praises of him who called*
> *you out of darkness into his wonderful light." (1 Peter 2:9 NIV)*

That day, the scriptures came alive. The lies I clung to for so long vanished. I sensed the grip of the evil influence over me loosening. I believed every truth of God's Word without a trace of questioning or doubt. Diving further into Scripture revealed much about what it means to be adopted into God's family and the power within my spiritual DNA. How could I possibly look at my family as champions, as the author spoke of? The further I read, the stronger my resolve grew to never return to the life I once lived.

For a long time, my identity was molded by my own choices and the legacies of those who came before me. It ended there in Borders. I recognized that I had to delve deeper to truly understand the depth of my trauma wounds.

Doing so intensified my curiosity about the lasting impact of the trauma I endured. Everything I read about the psychology behind such things did not give me much hope for a healthy future. The constant revictimization and self-destructive behaviors I had adopted only magnified the negative beliefs I harbored about myself and others. Getting to know myself and building a better life became my priority.

My research led me to the organization Darkness to Light. Not only did they advocate for victims of childhood sexual abuse, but they also equipped people through an advocate training program. Through this organization I learned how to identify signs of abuse in children and how important it is to use my voice for those who have no voice.

My writing exploded about the same time as my hunger for justice. My eyes were open now, and my brain began to make sense of why I would run from my crazy life at seventeen, try to bring the biker culture into my marriage at age twenty-five, and reclaim my roots again at age thirty-five. Serving as an agent of justice lit a fire in me. God also showed me that I belonged to Him and that all the things I've done would never cause Him to love me less.

When loneliness took hold of me, I remained intentional about not returning to self-destructive behavior. I made a solemn vow, declaring that men were strictly off-limits. I often found myself worshipping late at night. It chased the devil away on many occasions.

Knowing that my circle of friends was healthy and safe brought me peace of mind. With friends who held my soul's best interests close, everything changed for the better. God continued to amaze me on my recovery journey.

Though I never struggled with drug addiction, I learned something mind-boggling about recovery. Anyone can get something out of a recovery program. Relapse means returning to the place you swore you would never go again. Throwing myself away. Shame and guilt. Stealing. Lying. Isolation. I can't go there again. I won't.

One Sunday, our pastor mentioned Powerhouse Ministries, an organization that helps women through their recovery and even provides transitional housing for them and their children. While working in the church office one morning, I felt the Lord put Powerhouse on my heart. I pulled up their website and saw a job posting for a Transitional Living Center Facilitator. This sounds interesting. I called and left a message asking about the job. When they didn't call back, I gave up on the idea and moved on.

Two months later, after a couple job interviews, I still had not found a job. One Friday morning, I went to the local library to use their computer. I applied online for more than a dozen jobs. While packing up my paperwork, I remembered Powerhouse Ministries.

I logged back into the computer and completed their online job application. Heading to my car, my mind began to play games with me. The job probably isn't even available anymore. I turned on my cell phone to check my voicemail for messages. And I had one.

"Good morning, this is Donna Long with Powerhouse Ministries." I chuckled while listening to the rest of her message. "You called a couple months ago. I'm sorry it's taken me so long to get back to you. I'm wondering if you are still interested in the facilitator job. I'm here until noon today. I hope to hear back from you."

I called back immediately, but the phone went straight to voicemail. Darn! Now I have to wait until Monday!

Monday morning, my pastor greeted me at the door of the church office. "Cherie! Hey, you need to call Powerhouse Ministries."

I tilted my head, perplexed. "What? Did they call you looking for me?"

He looked surprised. "No. I happen to know they are looking for a bookkeeper. Are you still looking for a job?" When I told him what happened on Friday, he laughed and shook his head. "I think you better give them a call right away. Ask for Nancy and tell her I sent you."

Two days later, I interviewed with Nancy, the pastor at Powerhouse Ministries. She cast a look of deep compassion into my eyes after reading my resume. "Cherie, can I ask ... what happened to you?" She took me by surprise with her ways of searching my heart. But more than that, she cared about my life. Nancy offered me the bookkeeper position on the spot. Two weeks later, she offered a full-time opportunity which included writing grants. How awesome of God to use my passion for writing to do His work.

God also began working on Angelica's heart. I picked her up from school in the afternoons and brought her back to my office. Soon, she offered to help with filing and other tasks. When Powerhouse

Ministries partnered with Alternatives Pregnancy Center, Angelica shared with me how she wanted to help the pregnant teens who came in for counseling and prayer.

This held great significance for her. A deep yearning to help the young girls, mostly her age, flooded her heart. She told me, "Mom, when I look at them, I think of how that could be me."

Making God my focus led me on an adventure of a lifetime. He continued to show me He was not only my savior, but my husband, provider, protector, and best friend. He introduced me to Maribeth, a missionary whose passion for helping others radiated from her. She also served in the office at my church.

Knowing my circumstances, she offered to rent her home to me while she served on mission in Malawi. Those closest to me assured me my daughter would eventually begin to see the truth about her father and me. And she did.

The situation reversed, and my precious daughter expressed her desire to live with me permanently. In Maribeth's home, we found solace and security, a haven from the chaos of life. On weekends, Maribeth hosted her Bible study group. The moment you stepped into her home, a sense of calm washed over you, as if the Lord's peaceful presence permeated every corner. Watching my sister in Christ walk confidently in her identity as a child of God showed me the beauty and joy of a devoted life to the Lord. She discipled me in many ways.

Inviting my mother for a respite from Manuel at our new sanctuary came to an abrupt end when he showed up unannounced. He forced his way into the house in the middle of the night to take Mom home. The next day, Maribeth prayed through the house, rebuking the demonic spirits.

I realized the depth of my mistake when we sat for a talk with our pastor. Maribeth got right to the point. "Cherie, I need you to find another place to live before I leave for Malawi. I know you were trying to help your mom, but I can't leave knowing this sort of thing could happen again. And you are not strong enough to keep him away."

I could do nothing but apologize, my words heavy with remorse. I knew my friend was right. Manuel crashed my wedding and now he crashed our home. Chaos and dysfunction would continue to find their way into my life as long as my mother stayed with him.

I recognized the necessity of distancing myself from my mother and anyone who threatened my home and the path I chose. The most important thing was providing a safe home for my daughter.

In His perfect timing, the Lord provided the finances and an open door to rent our own two-bedroom condo. Living across the street from my daughter's high school saved me from the daily drive to and from school. The property manager, who I knew from my wild days, helped me out. A new tenant changed his mind on move-in day, so a unit came available the day I called.

Friends showered us with furniture and all the essentials. Angelica couldn't be happier that our place was close to her school. And I could rest easy not having to drive her to and from school.

Clearly, God showed us He was our good, good Father. That was critical because Angelica's dad would have nothing to do with her since she now lived with me full time.

It broke her heart, and it broke mine to see her in so much pain.

Chapter 20

Encouraging my daughter in her faith meant pointing out the enemy of her faith. And opportunities raised their ugly heads at every turn. I realized I could not approach faith the wrong way, forcing religious rules and regulations on her.

When God's hand moved or He showed up in some way, I'd simply point it out to her. The same thing applied with the manifestation of plain evil or opposition to God. As I walked on the spiritual training ground, I sensed the importance of passing along what I learned.

This became more evident when God planted in my heart a desire to work on the ministry side with the women in the transitional living center at Powerhouse. I started by leading a weekly Bible study. The women in the program trusted me because of the similarities we had in our pasts.

To guide others through The Genesis Process program in relapse prevention counseling, I had to go through the program myself. At first, I blew it off as a mere formality. But, how could I counsel women in the program without first understanding it myself? One of the leaders reviewed the workbook with me and encouraged me to remain honest with her and with myself. She added, "Cherie, this is going to take even more faith and courage. I'm here to support you, but you'll need to own some stuff."

With fearless determination, I embraced the intensity of The Genesis Process, ready to confront the challenges that lay ahead. This means I must share my secrets. It means telling her all those things I've never spoken out loud. To anyone. Oh God, there's no way I can do this on my own. You're going to have to do this.

The core of the program centered on changing how we respond to memories and emotions. I learned our limbic system, the core of our brain, is where our responses to life events are created and remembered. Lies about our identity originate there. I held an excess of lies to confront: Blood is thicker than water. I'm worthless. Nobody will ever truly love me. I'll never accomplish anything. I'll never change. I'll never fit in. I can only trust bikers.

Through denouncing the lies and praying biblical truths to replace them, I learned to cope in healthy ways. God rewired my thinking, replacing the imposters in my mind with His truth. When anxiety overwhelmed me, I now possessed the tools to help me identify the warning signs edging me toward relapse into codependency and relationship addiction. Rejection, abandonment, fear, and shame continued their attempt to torment my mind. The spiritual battle to keep me in bondage of my past raged on and required daily meditation of Scripture along with fervent prayers. During one Genesis session, I prayed this prayer.

God, I know you say all these wonderful things about me, but sometimes the world tries to drown them out. I'm chosen? I am yours? I'm a new creation? Created for a purpose? Lord, help me remain secure in my new identity. Deliver me from the orphan spirit. Help me hide my heart in yours. I feel like I'm holding on by a thread most of the time. My heart is clinging to you. I know I must cling only to you and your truth and promises. I am so grateful for all you are doing in my life, Jesus! Use me. Help me to stand strong so others may come to know you like I do. You are my husband and best friend. You alone are my Savior. Amen.

Completing The Genesis Process training forced me to come face to face with many things I didn't understand. When I shared about my recovery work with Pastor Jim at Lakeside Church, he invited me to join his leadership discipleship small group. He taught me a great deal about what it means to follow Christ. With Pastor Jim's faith in me, a sense of belonging and purpose rose within my soul. I experienced a profound shift in my self-perception. From there, I began to lead weekend ministry workshops for women and for those walking through the second half of their life.

I now understood that investing my time in the lives of hurting people also brought further healing and a renewed way of thinking and living my life. The women at Powerhouse longed for that same acceptance. Some of them were mandated by the court to complete the two-year recovery program as a condition of their parole. Others found sanctuary after having fled violent environments, while some came from the streets. Most suffered with addictions and were fighting for their life.

When a couple of the women asked me if I could lead a Bible study, I realized God led me to the right place. I clicked with the women. I understood them. It provided an opportunity to foster lasting friendships and a supportive community for the women after they graduated from the program.

I spread the word about the Bible study around my church and prayed, Lord, please soften the hearts of the women at my church.

Bring them here for fellowship and relationship. Help build bridges and tear down the walls of fear. Bind the spirit of condemnation. Bless our time together. You know who is meant to be here, Lord. Your will be done. In Jesus's name.

Sadly, none of the women from my church joined us. Discouragement occupied my thoughts. Then I remembered my prayer. God knew. I stood outside the entrance near the walkway connecting the living center and resource building on the Powerhouse Ministries campus. Maybe someone would show up.

Ten minutes before the start of the meeting, I spotted a nicely dressed woman walking from the living center. I greeted her with a big smile. "Hi there! Are you looking for our Bible study?"

She stopped while fumbling for her keys in her purse. Surprised, she said, "Oh … no. Uh, I just dropped off a meal for the ladies."

I stuck my hand out. "I'm Cherie. We're about to start our Bible study, Rick Warren's Forty Days of Love. Have you heard of it?"

The petite dark-haired woman, dressed in navy blue leggings and jacket introduced herself. Linda appeared apprehensive while continuing to reach for her keys. I backed up toward the door and waved her toward me. "Come on in. I'm sure the ladies would love to thank you for the delicious meal."

Linda not only took the time to meet the women, but before she left, she committed to joining us for the six-session study. And throughout the next several weeks, we encountered the exchange of tremendous love and compassion among all of us.

One evening, while closing up, Linda caught me alone before heading home. "You know, Cherie, I almost didn't join your group. Honestly, I felt intimidated at the thought of it. I mean, these women have lived hard lives. I didn't know what to think. I expected something different, I'm ashamed to admit. I'm so glad I stayed. I've never felt so comfortable. It's crazy, but my women's small group has been meeting together for over twenty years, and I've never shared the things I've shared here with you ladies. I feel so free. No, I feel safe. That's a better word. Thank you for inviting me."

Her confession floored me. Where I thought these women needed a mature Christian woman to mentor them, God used them to help her instead. Only God.

During my prayer time, I could not stop thinking about helping some of the women I ran with years ago. I tried to shake it off. How am I supposed to help them, Lord? I can't go back there alone. You wouldn't send me back alone. It's too dangerous.

When our group gathered again, I brought it up to the ladies. "Hey, I think Holy Spirit is telling me to minister to bikers." Each of them looked a bit confused. I mean, several of them came from the biker world. I clarified, "Returning to my old stomping grounds is what I meant." We all agreed it's best to do what God is asking us to do.

I knew I couldn't go running back to that neighborhood. Not as a single woman. Not alone. When I said dangerous, I meant it. The devil fed on my weaknesses and threw temptation my way the moment I'd take a stand for the Lord.

A blatant example is when a tall, handsome, rugged man caught my eye while taking care of a traffic ticket at the courthouse. We made eye contact and sensed an overwhelming physical attraction to each other. Throughout the two hours there, we chatted in line and sat together in the courtroom.

During the first minutes of engaging with the man, I remember blurting, "There has got to be a bigger reason for Jesus to have me here—I just know it." In my giddy state, talking about Jesus seemed appropriate. During our small talk, I continued mentioning the Lord. I sensed shame when he looked down at the floor, confessing he had not stepped into a church in over twenty-five years. In my attempt to ease his mind, I said, "Well, you do not have to go to church to have a relationship with Jesus."

Our eyes and smiles continued to connect after pleading our cases before the judge. It was apparent that he was attracted to my constant mention of Jesus, wasn't it? Afterward, I waited for him in the crowded lobby area. With every seat taken, I chose a spot across from the seating area and checked my phone messages.

A faint, feeble voice called across the room, "Excuse me, miss?" I looked over to see a small, frail, older woman waving her cane at me. She sweetly repeated, "Yes, miss? Can you come help me?"

Gesturing to my chest, I mouthed, "Who, me?"

She nodded with a gentle smile.

I walked across the lobby of chairs and sofas filled with at least thirty people to get to the woman. I admired her elegant long gray wool coat trimmed in black fur. She adjusted her vintage hat, adorned with netting and feathers, to sit perfectly on her head.

She asked, "Would you be so kind to walk me to the ladies' room?" She held her cane up with her right hand. "My cane helps me on this side, but I need support for my other side."

I glanced around at all the other people sitting right beside her. Why she did not ask one of the people seated next to her seemed rather strange. My thoughts shifted to the man I wanted to invite for coffee. "Uh … Yes, of course." I helped her from her seat, supporting her left arm.

On our way through the corridor of the courthouse, she shared praises of Jesus healing her kidneys, her heart, and praised Him for her new hip. Her delight in the Lord continued all the way to the restroom. We shared praises through the stall door. All the way back to the lobby, she never stopped praising Jesus. I thought of the irony.

The beautiful woman blessed me in the name of Jesus after I helped her to her seat. After a couple of minutes, I noticed my friend in the courtroom was done and gone. I yelled at God when I got back to my car. Pounding on the steering wheel, I wanted answers. "So what was that all about? I finally feel safe enough to welcome a man into my life, and he disappears?" When I finished my little tantrum, I inhaled, then exhaled.

The Lord spoke into my heart, He would have done you harm. My soul calmed with the realization that God orchestrated it all. It seemed the deeper and stronger my relationship grew and the more I devoted my body and my heart to God, the more spiritual resistance I encountered. However, there were clear and undeniable manifestations of God's protection.

The challenge of venturing into the wilderness, following Jesus, and rebuilding my life did not come without bouts of anxiety, loneliness, rejection, depression, and other aftereffects of the trauma from my past. Jesus, I promise to remain pure and trust you as my husband. Draw me deeper into your heart so I may be protected and hidden in you.

While I understood God had my back, He also removed fear of the devil.

After three straight days of illness, I quarantined myself in my bedroom while Kari Jobe's "Revelation Song" played on repeat. I stayed up late and shared the music video on social media. No sooner had I posted it, than a private message from a man, who shared a mutual friend with me, appeared in my inbox.

"What makes you think your Jesus even hears you? Who do you think you are? Your faith will do you no good."

No stranger to the spirit of intimidation, I typed my response, "Get behind me, Satan. You can go right back to the pit of hell."

Block.

During that night and over the course of those three days leading to Passover, I came to understand how powerful worship is when Satan is prowling around. And he is always prowling around. While I had prior knowledge of spiritual warfare, the lie aimed at me through the man in that private message stood out as it was a deliberate one-on-one encounter, rather than a mere presence in my circumstances. When I followed up with Pastor Jim about it the following week, he helped me understand that I had become a direct threat, and the devil was no longer holding back.

But prior to the evil message during Passover, the Holy Spirit had begun equipping me with spiritual discernment and came to my defense. I felt a divine presence as God prepared me. His intention was to not only expand my knowledge, but also deepen my understanding of the spiritual realm. I clung to the cross, my only source of true protection and peace.

I had to while the Lord led me into an unfamiliar season of singleness. Not belonging to any one person overwhelmed me at times. In my loneliness, I fought thoughts of picking up the phone to call Lefty. In recovery, I learned about unhealthy soul ties and how to sever them. My recovery required me to do many things I never imagined I'd ever do, including distancing myself from my own family. Repentance required me to turn away from ungodly relationships, immoral behavior, and idols.

The thought kept tugging at me to return to club territory to witness to the biker sisters. My soul hurt for them. If only I could help them discover what I found in Christ, a way out of bondage.

Learning about Christian motorcycle ministries intrigued me. I spent time online researching local biker ministries. It was as though my prayer was heard and answered, confirming that God didn't mean for me to face this alone.

One of my friends on social media suggested I connect with Johnny Lujan, leader of a local chapter of Black Sheep Harley-Davidsons for Christ, a motorcycle ministry in the mission field of Harley Owners Group (HOG) members. Johnny invited me to join them for breakfast before they headed out for a ride. This led to an open invitation to attend their events and regular breakfast gatherings. It reminded me how much I missed riding. Though I enjoyed meeting Cristian bikers, I felt vulnerable when I joined them at biker rallies. I could not let my guard down.

Balancing ministry and work at Powerhouse with my life as a single mom left little time to attend motorcycle ministry events. Writing grant proposals at work increased my passion for writing my own work. I submitted a piece of poetry to a new local biker magazine, *Thunder Roads Magazine NorCal*. To my surprise, I got published. This boosted my confidence as a writer and led me to enroll in the Jerry B. Jenkins Christian Writers Guild.

When Pastor Johnny showed up at my office while I worked late, I sensed God was up to something. By chance, he was next door working for a client when he noticed the Powerhouse Ministries sign and remembered that I worked there.

We met in the office lobby and talked for roughly an hour about all the things God placed on my heart about ministering to the club sisters I used to party with at The Tumbleweed in Rancho Cordova. When I expressed my concern about going alone, he said, "Well, you know, that's funny, because my partner George and I were talking about doing the Lord's work somewhere along the Highway 50 corridor. Maybe plant a biker church."

The idea of launching a biker church filled me with exhilaration and anticipation. "That's exciting. We really need a church for bikers. They understand each other, and bikers don't need anyone else judging them with glares and stares. Churches say to come as you are, but that's not how it works most times. This is what we contend with here at Powerhouse. Many women from these local churches are afraid to engage with the women here." Pastor Johnny agreed and prayed with me before he left.

God set the planning in motion over the next couple of weeks. One of the biker sisters from the Powerhouse transition center expressed interest in the new ministry. Sabrina joined me at our first church plant prayer meeting with Pastor Johnny and Pastor George at a local restaurant. We all shared God's vision for a biker church and began driving along the Highway 50 corridor through Rancho Cordova, praying for a place to gather.

Planting a church for those rejected by society became another way to build bridges. Many often feel rejected by God because of a moral failure. I once knew the hopeless feeling of considering oneself beyond redemption, like sinking into a dark, bottomless pit.

The owner, a devout Christian, of the nearby Jimboy's Tacos always greeted us with a warm smile. When he heard about our quest to find a place to hold church, he invited us to meet in his parking lot. We could not ask for a better location.

Bikers rode up and down Folsom Boulevard day and night. Where bikes gather, more bikers come. Some showed up in their club colors to find out what was going on. One brother approached me and asked why we gathered in the parking lot and not in a building. The patch on his cut read "Digger." His whole demeanor shifted when I mentioned we were waiting for the Lord's guidance. Digger scratched his head and nodded, wide-eyed. "I don't know the Lord, but I sure know about the devil."

His statement caught me by surprise. "Oh, really?" Intrigued, I said, "Go on."

Folding his thin, tatted arms, Digger shifted his stance. "I was fried." Shaking his head, he broke our eye contact. "I did so much crank, I could barely breathe. I think I had a seizure." Digger looked at my face. His eyes grew intense and telling. "All I know is the devil showed his face. Scared me straight. I thought I was in hell." He nodded, his voice shaky with emotion. "Not sure how I'm standing here with you right now."

I knew Digger wasn't just one of the lucky ones. It didn't matter that he didn't know the Lord. Jesus rescued him. I discerned my new friend was looking for answers. So, I told him. "Jesus rescued you. That's how you're standing here. He rescued me too." I sensed he was struggling with shame, so I asked Digger if I could pray with him, his eyes revealing the pain he carried. Pastor Johnny walked up, introduced himself, and we prayed over our friend.

This was why God put this ministry on my heart. A disturbance in my soul set in when I thought about popping in at the Tumbleweed with invitations to join us. That check in my spirit held me back. How else am I going to reach those girls if I don't go, Lord?

As the Fall evenings grew colder, we found shelter for our gatherings at a nearby mini storage. Johnny and George knew a business owner who ran things out of a large storage unit. He offered to open the doors on one side of the unit to make room for us and did not mind the dozens of bikes parked out front.

We named our little church Thunder Road Biker Church. We held fundraising events with pancake breakfasts and partnered with local businesses. God began blessing our church as finances flowed into the ministry. This allowed us to sign a lease for indoor space where we could hang a sign. Fifty people began calling Thunder Road Biker Church home.

One night, while scrolling through Facebook posts, Penny, a blast from my past, appeared in my feed. My heart raced recalling our last interaction. I did not fear Penny, just the dangerous men she associated with. I froze in panic when I discovered Sabrina was best friends with Penny's daughter, Maria. What have I done, inviting Sabrina into my life outside of Powerhouse? Penny cannot know where I live. My daughter's in danger. Breathe, Cherie. The devil is only taunting you.

I dug around Penny's profile and saw a photo of her friend who threatened to rape me There he is. It's not safe.

I closed my eyes to calm myself. A familiar sense of peace calmed my spirit. I felt God assuring me. My plans are for good, not for evil. I invited you to the banquet. Why not her? It'd been five years. Maybe things had changed. I reached out through social media and reconnected. Penny nearly lost her life in recent months from an aggressive blood infection. She, too, left her old life behind. When we met for coffee, we shared tears, past hurts, and understanding. I ended up picking her up every Thursday evening so she could be a part of our biker church family.

Many of our Thunder Road brothers and sisters shared stories that made me shudder. To gain their trust and hear the worst of the worst, along with accounts of the miraculous, the air in the church seemed charged with divine purpose.

I had further confirmation of this when I made a stop at the nearby gas station before a weekend fundraising event. The cashier recognized me right away. It took me a moment, but then I recalled she was the wife of one of the brothers from the Misplaced Souls motorcycle club. Barbara asked that I come back at the end of her shift so we could catch up. That evening, I prayed with her and invited her to Thunder Road.

These reconnections continued with women from my past. The Lord sent a clear message that He did not want me returning to the biker bar. He had everything under control and never asked me to walk into the lion's den.

Pastor Johnny believed sharing my testimony with our Thunder Road family was a good idea. So, one day, four months after we launched our little church, I stood before fifty or so bikers, testifying to all I had witnessed and sharing the gospel. This in and of itself was miraculous because in the male-dominated biker culture, women were property, even today.

I'm not sure why I was so surprised to see God break through those barriers. I recognized when God calls us to lead in the most difficult areas, the enemy does not have a chance, because God is our true source of strength. He always made a way to accomplish the work He set out to do.

Amidst the new ministry, my recovery journey continued to unfold, forcing me to confront challenging decisions that felt over-whelming to face alone.

Chapter 21

Part of taking responsibility for my healing was understanding how my woundedness had affected various aspects of my life including the people close to me. In my research, I learned about the Adverse Childhood Experiences study (ACEs). The study, conducted by Kaiser Permanente and the Centers for Disease Control, focused on how traumatic childhood events increased the risk of health problems later in life. The data also provided insights into the behavioral impact. As the ACE score increases, the behavioral impact becomes more severe. I realized the severity of my situation when I scored eight out of ten ACEs, putting me at the highest risk.

I also joined a faith-based twelve-step group at Lakeside Church which focused on emotional healing. The curriculum helped me unearth lingering, hidden wounds that were still influencing my relapse. While I learned about making amends, I knew I needed to take ownership of my part in the demise of my marriage. I hesitated to dial my ex's phone number. All he can do is hang up on me.

Surprisingly, Todd allowed me the time to say what I needed to say. "I want you to know how sorry I am for my role in the destruction of our marriage. I'm not going to make any excuses. I didn't know how to handle everything going on inside of me."

He considered it water under the bridge. We found common ground with the goal of making things easier on our daughter.

A ton of bricks lifted from my soul. The sudden shift was nothing short of amazing. Angelica found our reconciliation astounding, but it brought her relief.

Making amends was just one part of my journey. Everything that happened was truly the work of God. The people in my life played a crucial role in speaking truth about who I was and providing a ton of help. Looking at myself from God's point of view shifted my perception. Navigating life became much easier with my newfound self-worth and the knowledge that God had my back. He became my compass, my true north.

Staying true to my beliefs required boundaries—a new concept I learned through counseling. Boundaries with myself. And with others. Setting boundaries allowed me to honor my values, goals, and needs instead of avoiding rejection. Boundaries kept me on the path God had for my life. This newfound way of life often felt hostile as I fought for my right to a better life for me and Angelica.

Much of my family continued living the lifestyle I no longer felt comfortable around. To remain focused on my recovery and the changes God had for me, I could not associate with anyone who smoked pot or mocked God in any way. My soul could not tolerate being in the company of anyone who reminded me of my abusers or the events from my past.

The atmosphere at work grew tense and unsettling. The decrease in donor contributions had an impact on the operational budget. Grant funding helped some, but not enough. Rather than find another job, I hung on. I knew well that I should leave, but the fear of voluntarily releasing the stability of full-time work paralyzed me. The angst in my gut would not go away. I even said something to one of my coworkers while confiding to her in my office. "I think God has something else for me."

Her response was spot on. "Do you think that's very wise to ignore what God is telling you to do?"

Within a matter of months, volunteers took over my job, as well as two other positions. Hindsight revealed my inability to discern what God was telling me to do. Either that, or I was too afraid to listen. I couldn't trust my judgment.

Fear continued to grip me in waves. I threw caution to the wind and took a road trip with my daughter and niece before looking for work again. Giving up my apartment was the only choice I had once my severance ran out.

Reckless behavior taunted me at Thunder Road. I read that God never tempts us. He will test us, but never tempt us. One night, while standing outside in the parking lot full of motorcycles, desire to ride welled up in me while I admired the men putting on their gear.

One man showed up solo every Thursday night. Where is he? I scouted through the bikes and spotted him at the end of the row. My heart quickened. There he was. Should I say hello? It felt like I was the only one standing there. The desire to jump on the back of his bike and race off overwhelmed my thoughts. I stepped toward him, but he fired up his bike and left. Disappointment took hold. Then I remembered the day in the courthouse. Yes, Lord. You provide a way out of every temptation. Distraction is the last thing I need. That night, I prioritized my livelihood, my daughter, and my recovery.

While navigating the changes in my work and looking for a place to live, my mother helped me out with finances, but my daughter and I had no family to stay with temporarily. I reached out to friends for their support. The Lord made sure we were never on the streets. Over the next six months, three generous friends opened their homes to us.

I believed God wanted me to continue writing grants for non-profits who were doing His work. So, I did pro bono work for organizations that helped rescue girls from sex trafficking, supporting wounded soldiers and their families, and a crisis pregnancy center. Most nonprofits looking for funding did not have the finances to pay a grant writer.

By the grace of God, a door opened for a human resources position at a local startup company. Knowing I could afford rent again, I contacted my previous property manager. Within two weeks, Angelica and I returned to the same condo I had reluctantly given up less than a year ago. The Lord revealed that He himself kept the door to our condo open and available for us. He turned our months of transition into a blessing for not only me, but for those who graciously provided us with a place to stay.

After recovering from the turmoil of homelessness, I sensed a nudge from the Lord, as if He summoned me to meet with Him at the ocean. Returning to the coast for solitude with the Lord was my favorite since that is where I met Him for the first time. When I sensed the whisper grow in intensity, arrangements were set in motion. There was a special conversation I wanted to have with Him concerning my soul mate. A friend suggested I get specific with God about what I'd like in a husband.

Eager to escape the summer heat, I packed my bag the day before my planned getaway. While packing, the Holy Spirit nudged Monica to call me with an invitation to a women's conference which started that Sunday evening in Seaside. I no longer believed in coincidences. God had something for me there and it was urgent.

For the first time, I had a heart to heart with the Lord about my soul mate. Lying in the sand, I wrote my letter to Jesus about my future husband. May his faith and identity in you be unwavering. He will be the spiritual authority in our home. His love and compassion will draw others to You. "Protect him, Jesus. When he seeks You, may he walk in obedience to the way You call him so he may find me. Guide his steps and let his heart hear mine. Amen."

Before heading home, our conference speaker shared a word specially for me: "You are His jewel and called to show forth His glory. You shine because of what the Lord has put in you. Release your faith to receive the Lord's abundant provision. Your reward in heaven will be those who you led to Jesus. They will be jewels in your crown."

The following week, I received a substantial pay increase which allowed us a nicer place to live. But, shortly following our move, everything began to unravel with my job when investors announced a company merger. Again, Lord? How can this be happening yet again?

My assistant, a longtime believer, and I prayed together in my office. I paid special attention when she said, "Please do not allow one single day in gap of employment for Cherie."

While the merger took place, my focus was on getting a job with a large health care company. Their job postings bombarded the online career boards. Everything required a degree I did not have. Well, I guess I shot myself in the foot by not getting my degree. There's no chance. No sense in torturing myself any longer.

After I revamped my résumé, I uploaded it to a popular online site. Within an hour, I received a call from a recruiter. She told me she found the perfect position for me … with the health care company I'd hoped to work for. I filled her in on giving up on them. Within two months, without one day in gap of employment, I started working for them.

During this time, the Lord spoke to my heart. It is I who determines your worth and your promotion. Living out my devotion to Jesus and trusting Him with my life came with great reward. Nobody ever explained that many of God's promises are conditional. I discovered this while studying Psalm 37:

> *"Trust in the LORD and do good; dwell in the land and enjoy safe pasture. Take delight in the LORD, and he will give you the desires of your heart. Commit your way to the LORD; trust in him and he will do this: He will make your righteous reward shine like the dawn, your vindication like the noonday sun. Be still before the LORD and wait patiently for him." (Psalm 37:3–7 NIV)*

If I continued to devote all I did to God and continued becoming His beloved, He would shape my life according to these promises. I prayed, "Lord, help change my desires so that I may continue to be made new. My allegiance is with you. I trust you. I will always glorify you. Use me, God. Make some sense out of it all. I commit everything I do for your glory. Let your justice continue to shine over my life. Help me stand strong. Thank you for going to battle for me and for your protection. Thank you for my little writing sanctuary too! Amen."

As my career advanced, I sensed a restlessness in my spirit. Although I adored my job, I came to the realization that my true passion for writing was being pushed aside. God reminded me to write.

I bought an inexpensive writing desk and placed it under my window in my bedroom. The words flowed from my keyboard, igniting a burning determination within me to publish my story. The nudge in my spirit reminded me of the dream when the Lord told me: Tell them.

This feeling grew into a conviction. My heart overflowed with joy at every opportunity to share my story at women's groups and speaking engagements.

Even though I was on the right track in life, Satan's persistent assault on my mind never ceased. He took advantage of my weakened state caused by past trauma triggers. Planting thoughts of doubt and rejection was his favorite strategy. Fortunately, I understood the enemy's goal to attack my identity with emotional baggage and negative feelings about myself, other people, and God. Discovering true belonging came only after I completely trusted my identity as God's beloved daughter.

Loneliness and self-rejection continued to creep up from time to time. But God's relentless love reminded me of my true belonging as His beloved. Speaking and declaring myself as chosen and beloved, a critical spiritual discipline, kept the enemy at bay.

Jesus rescued me from the depths of the dead sea, breathing new life into me as His beloved. He took my hand as my protector, husband, best friend, provider, and savior. Through worship, His presence would often surge, bringing loving reminders that ministered to my soul.

To overcome bouts of loneliness, I engaged with a community of fellow believers. I expected us to be one big family. As a single mother in need of constant help, I often felt like part of their local mission field. The early church consisted of genuine fellowship. They did life together. What was I missing? Was this the result of my own self-inflicted wounds of rejection and alienation? I wondered if Thunder

Road Biker Church was the sole place where I'd ever experience a genuine sense of belonging.

That belonging was more than the revelation of myself as God's beloved. I discovered that belonging well and becoming His beloved required living a life of worship through the use of my passions and gifts. Searching my soul, I founded my nonprofit, The Justice Writer Group. My mission was to support faith-based organizations whose mission centered around social justice. Most of these agents of justice struggled with funding. God placed it upon my heart to use my grant writing experience and passion for His justice to locate resources for them.

In February 2012, I jumped at the opportunity to attend the first Justice Conference in Portland, Oregon. The event, sponsored by World Relief, drew thirty-five hundred attendees from forty-one states and twenty countries, including ministries, churches, and nonprofits. I set out to gain knowledge about worldwide social justice initiatives and to connect with nonprofits in need of grant services.

I looked forward to hearing author and pastor, Francis Chan's message on social justice. To my surprise, it was Richard Twiss, a Native American pastor, author, and community leader, who made the greatest impact over the two-day conference. Twiss's fervor for social justice was deeply rooted in his desire to better integrate Native American culture with Christian worship. He described his experience with Christian groups and their mission work on the reservations. His reference "You Christians" offended some. But I understood his frustration and hurt.

Twiss shared his plea with the predominantly Christian audience. "We don't want your charity. We want your brotherhood. Why not join us at our powwow after painting our buildings, planting flowers, or bringing us food? Get to know who we are. Understand we love Jesus as you do, but we have a different way of showing it."

Twiss's presentation made a deep imprint upon my heart. Not so much for my friend seated next to me. Throughout his speech, she uttered how offensive his statements were to her. She was livid, finding it hard to accept that the conference directors would permit such a message to be spread from the platform. Incidentally, while we waited for our next keynote, Twiss sat in the chair on the other side of my friend.

Later that evening, she shared all about her Jesus moment. "You know, as soon as that man sat next to me, God started dealing with my attitude. I know Twiss wasn't pointing a finger at me from the stage."

I tried to understand why she and I had such different reactions to Twiss's words. I explained my take from his message. "He spoke from a place of longing to belong and not to be treated as an outsider… like a charity case."

Reflecting on the conversation with my friend, I gained insight that some individuals have never known the sting of rejection that accompanies life on the fringes of society. The conference reignited my passion more than ever before, surpassing the time my pastor discouraged my efforts to train church staff on child abuse awareness.

My aha moment was discovering that the perceived rejection I experienced from my pastor allowed the Lord to redirect me. This was the perfect opportunity to establish a network of nonprofits to use my grant writing skills for the kingdom. I thanked God for leading me into a much larger territory.

The rebranding of my soul continued to unfold with a change of perspective on purpose, relationships, priorities, and what I believed about myself. My understanding of devotion and belonging, then versus now, replaced all obligation or allegiance to man with the divine providence of God.

The devil understood he couldn't get to my soul. Instead, family relationships became more divided through differences in our lifestyle, demonic influence, and unresolved wounds.

The enlightenment I gained from my connection with things of God revealed the enemy's tactics, as I witnessed others being manipulated to pass judgment and condemnation onto me. Satan loved to cast shame and distract me from truth. Remaining focused on God's Word became my anchor. Holy Spirit spoke to my heart, conquering the cursing lies of the devil.

Something settled in my heart when I overheard Angelica on the phone with a girlfriend say, "Tell your mom she doesn't have anything to worry about. My mom is an overzealous Christian."

What a compliment! I'll take on that label. I smiled inside with a prayer. Wow, my little girl sees you, Lord. Thank you. I want her to know you too. Nothing or nobody will come before Angelica. She is your gift and is my ministry for now.

Every time I saw God's hand in something, I'd point it out to my daughter. I felt a sense of belonging as I immersed myself in the presence of God. I was His beloved daughter, basking in His unconditional love. I no longer cared about pleasing anyone and had no intention of seeking approval from others.

My allegiance was like a devotion to the heavens. In my quiet time, I read about my worth. It reinforced what I'd seen God do in my life. With unwavering determination, I centered my efforts on becoming God's best and embracing His divine plan for me.

My heart found contentment in Christ alone. Life was not meant to be lived alone; it is a symphony of connections and relationships.

Over time, as thoughts of marriage came up, I prayed about it. God made room in my heart for a purpose mate. During my quiet time with the Lord one night, He spoke to my heart. You will not have to go looking for a husband. He will show up at your front door. You will know him.

I continued to hide my heart in His. That's the place where God's best would find me. No impostor would suffice. Only the real deal. I gained a clear understanding of what was right and wrong in dating. I couldn't understand why my old thought patterns occasionally resurfaced in my mind. All the Scriptures I studied mentioned being made a new creation, the old has passed away, or we will walk in the newness of life. My new life wasn't an instant transformation, but rather a collection of small moments and choices to embrace. I chased after where I saw God's spirit moving.

My friend, Janet Thompson, wrote in her book, *Everyday Brave: Living Courageously as a Woman of Faith*, "Modern-day demons can take residence in a soul and spirit when dabbling in the occult or satanic rituals, but they can also present themselves in the form of oppressive addictions or chronic sin with drugs, alcohol, sex, perversion, pornography, food, money, theft, or more. When addictions replace God as first place in a life, the devil gets a foothold into the victim's mind, heart, and soul, and let's those demons—Satan's emissaries—fill the void on the throne of a life where only God should rule."

Having a group of solid Christians in my inner circle helped me stay on track. Remaining anchored in God's word was vital because it was through Holy Spirit the Word of God came alive, healing, guiding, transforming, and loving me. That is how I learned Christians were not perfect.

Much like myself, Christians were a community of flawed individuals in need of a savior.

Chapter 22

The same revelation came to me regarding men. The more I examined my life choices, the more I realized a pattern of falling for imposters. I, too, suffered from a more common form of imposter syndrome, where I welcomed physical, psychological, and spiritual imposters with open arms and a deceived heart.

After five years, I put my toes in the water again and began browsing Christian dating sites. I discovered there are predators everywhere, Christian sites included. Danny seemed like a nice guy. His profile stated he was a Christian. After one date, I knew Danny did not understand the meaning of following Christ.

I found out the hard way this was the case with most of the men who professed their belief in God. I became tired of meeting imposters. It seemed like I had a magnetic pull, drawing them toward me.

That was my version of imposter syndrome, I had it, alright. Collecting imposters. The fact is the enemy often sent them my way to seduce me and lure me away from God's best. All I wanted was to meet a Christian man who understood the meaning of having a relationship with Jesus.

Tired of imposters, I jumped online to cancel my dating site subscription. That proved no simple task, even for someone as technologically inclined as me. While unsubscribing to a site, a notification pinged. I took a peek.

Interesting. No profile picture? I paused. What the heck. Click. His profile read, "I WANT TO MEET A WOMAN WHO KNOWS WHAT IT TRULY MEANS TO HAVE A RELATIONSHIP WITH JESUS!!! AND I WANT TO MAKE HER LAUGH EVERY DAY!!!"

I appreciated this guy's boldness. And Mike definitely grabbed my attention with his loud digital voice and exclamation marks. So, we connected. When he provided a photo, we talked on the phone. Within two weeks, he showed up at my front door, fulfilling what I heard from the Lord.

I knew he was the man God prepared for me to marry. After one year and ten months, we married at Mission Springs, on the very altar where I gave my heart to Jesus. Now, I could fully immerse myself in writing for the Lord without any distractions. I believed God wanted me to know He would always protect me and use my husband to fulfill the dream He gave me to tell them.

And the full revelation came from the other dream where I could not find my way through the fog. The Holy Spirit spoke while journaling on our honeymoon. "Only I could rescue you from the darkness. Seek me to find your way. It was I who provided a safe way out. Todd would never become the spiritual leader and embrace the plan I have for you."

God clearly brought us together as purpose mates. The Bible says, "Blessed is she who has believed that the Lord would fulfill his promises to her" (Luke 1:45 NIV). Our union is like a richly detailed novel, filled with moments of joy, struggle, and triumph. Living authentically brought a sense of inner peace, fulfillment, and alignment with my true self. God would not have me live unknown as an imposter. After all, Cherie, the name given to me at birth, means Beloved.

Marrying Mike was like a tapestry of answered prayers coming together in perfect harmony. He was the oldest of five siblings, with one in heaven. His parents married as teens and their marriage continued to thrive well after sixty years. Marrying into the Denna family was one of the greatest honors of my life. They take care of each other. Mike ensured his parents would never have to concern themselves with the later years of their life together.

As God arranged it, Mike lived in a historical farmhouse only a mile away from where Angelica had attended high school. I remembered driving down that street years before he acquired the property and five years before we met. Admiring the charming farmhouses lining the country road, scattered with orchards here and there, I thought that it sure would be nice to grow old with someone in one of these farmhouses. We could sit in on our wrap-around deck and watch the sunset from our rocking chairs.

When he first showed me where he lived, I knew the Lord gave me that vision, as a dream, or maybe a promise. Only God knew what was to come.

Within months after getting married, Mike's esophagus ruptured, and he began hemorrhaging. A female neighbor rushed to my door when the paramedics carried my husband out on the gurney. She cried, "Please let me know if there is anything I can do."

She was so sweet to offer. We only knew one another in passing. I prayed all the way to the hospital and through his emergency surgery. Lord, this can't be happening. We haven't even celebrated our first anniversary. Please save my husband. You brought him to me for a purpose. Protect him, please.

I contacted every prayer warrior I could think of to storm the gates of heaven. They admitted my husband to the ICU while still heavily anesthetized. Sitting at his bedside, I held Mike's hand. His eyes fluttered open, and he immediately felt the weight and pressure on his chest. I blinked away my tears and smiled with relief, locking eyes with him.

Slowly regaining consciousness, my husband carefully traced the letters "JESUS" on the bedsheet with his index finger.

Joy, admiration, and gratitude all welled up in me. I squeezed my husband's hand, "Yes, love, Jesus is with us."

A day or so later, Mike's respiratory therapist came to begin treatment. She instantly recognized us and pulled down her protective mask. God orchestrated my neighbor to help Mike, just as she had offered days before.

Over the course of the next two weeks, my husband's condition worsened with a full-blown infection and double pneumonia. Mike's survival was described by two doctors as nothing short of a miracle. I was in awe of how the Lord made His presence known throughout our time at the hospital. That included how our church family and Mike's family pulled together to move us from my condo into our house.

My husband and I dedicated our home to the Lord's work. A huge part of that was providing a safe place for Mike's parents. Our home was a vessel for the Lord's blessings, and though we were unsure of the specifics, our hearts were receptive and ready. Mike suggested I use the upstairs space for my writing. He also insisted I register for a writers' conference. He understood the magnitude of remaining obedient to God's calling on my life. For both of us.

During the writing of my hard story, a swarm of triggers resurfaced while revisiting past trauma. The onslaught of dark thoughts and emotions took me by surprise. I confided in my pastor, "I thought I had forgiven already."

His wise words helped me realize that even though I had forgiven, there was still a lingering sense of grief within me. "It's not easy looking down at a lifetime of trauma. You walked through each episode and survived one trauma at a time. Now, you're reliving all of it at once." He reminded me to write from a place of victory and to keep in mind the possibility of forgiving all over again. The recollection of my encounters with the Holy Spirit became a key factor in my ability to defend against spiritual warfare.

My husband and I sat with my pastor at our dining room table sharing about times Holy Spirit left us in awe. I described one example of when I volunteered to photograph our church baptisms. "I had no idea what I was getting into. I've never felt God's presence so powerfully—it's truly ethereal and incredible. While he prayed over each person, I prayed and snapped a shot. Following that, I captured the moment they were immersed into the water and another when they emerged."

Pastor Michael shook his head. "Wow, Cherie. I've baptized a good number of people, so I know what a gift that must have been for you."

I pondered the holy moments I had the honor to witness. "This is the very thing that compels me to write. I want everyone to know that Holy Spirit is real."

My pastor nodded and smiled through my testimony. He knew. Baptisms were his business. "Cherie, you've got this. You know when the enemy is trying to trick you into believing his lies. You're doing great."

Meeting with our pastor and remaining mindful of my thoughts helped combat imposter syndrome. However, one night while writing about the intensity of spiritual warfare, I decided to completely redefine the concept of imposter syndrome. Rather than identifying myself as the imposter, I captured the internal lies and toxic thoughts and labeled them the imposters. I could no longer allow the imposters to take up space in my mind, spirit, and soul.

Armed with a deeper understanding of how these imposters operate, I felt compelled to protect my mom. Wherever I lived, I tried to offer my home as a haven for my mother when Manuel was on a rampage. Over the years, I prayed for her to walk away. She tried a few times but fell prey to his manipulation and went right back to him after two weeks. My husband assured my mom that she always had a safe place to live with us.

The final time Manuel kicked my mom out of their home, she chose to stay at a friend's house not far from Manuel's house. When she took a serious fall, down the steps of her friend's carport, I drove to San Jose and brought her home from the hospital to recover.

The severity of her concussion and other injuries required me to assume the roll of her full-time advocate and caregiver. To compound things, I learned my mom's friend helped her secure a restraining order to keep Manuel away from where she was staying. For once, Mom had the legal backing to keep Manuel from intruding into our home. But, it required more of my attention with all the legal red tape and hearings.

After a few months, she agreed to make her new home with Mike and me. The intense emotional ride she endured while confronting her deep-seated attachment to a narcissist over forty-two years eventually led her to a profound self-discovery. The blessing was my mother lived in a place where her livelihood was no longer threatened. My hope was for my mom to live in peace for once in her life.

Of course, God had an even bigger plan for my mom and me. While I worked on my book, my mom helped me remember certain details, but her opinions and justifications were clearly distorted. Especially when talking about Van. I never expected our soul wounds to clash so violently. Her trauma responses triggered mine which created tremendous discord in our home.

Mike comforted me one night when I confided in him, saying, "Maybe it's best to keep your writing discussions separate from your mom. Revisiting those years could be a painful experience for her too."

But there was a deeper disturbance in my mom's spirit. She carried tremendous rage and struggled to contain it. With God's help, she worked through forgiveness and started seeing herself as beloved, even amid brokenness. Of course, this was only barely touching the extent of Mom's healing to come after enduring a lifetime of abuse and indescribable loss. But at least she was no longer subjected to ongoing emotional abuse. She also had people around her who watched out for her wellbeing.

Gradually, through prayers and tears, the peace of the Lord healed our hearts and led my mom on a remarkable transformation. After eighteen months, peace settled in her heart as her mind found renewal, and she discovered newfound freedom in the sanctuary of her own apartment. Mom's favorite feature of her new place was the deck that overlooked a man-made pond.

One morning, we drank our coffee and fed the ducks and geese gathered at her deck. My mom beamed at me as only a mother can. "Honey, I want to thank you for helping me see what love is supposed to look like." Her words had a profound, spiritual effect on my heart. "I wake up every morning and listen to Brandon Lake's song, Gratitude."

Mom was the happiest I'd seen her. She enjoyed joining us at church and eventually learned how to incorporate healthy boundaries into her life. Witnessing my mom stand up for herself against manipulation highlighted the Lord's transformation in her. She continued to talk about how much she wanted to share gratitude with our family. The peace in her heart was the most valuable thing she had to offer.

Sorting through memories with my mom, I reflected on the painful events from my past and marveled at the strength that propelled me forward. How did I muster the bravery as a little girl to speak about sexual abuse in my childhood? Where did I find the energy to keep going? Why wasn't I ever trafficked? How did I not end up kidnapped and murdered? How did I not die of a drug overdose or get sick with STDs? Why did I not plunge over that icy mountain canyon?

I never really expected an answer to my questions. I believe what the Bible says in Romans 8:28 (NIV), "And we know that in all things God works for the good of those who love him, who have been called according to his purpose."

The Lord crafted a special message for me while preparing to write about my most traumatic childhood memory. And on of all days, August 28, Van's birthday. I certainly didn't plan it that way. I know God did though. The month of August proved to bring major life altering events, many of which rocked my world. Remaining proactive and planning something positive for myself, I reserved a room at the Pigeon Point Lighthouse Hostel. I returned to the ocean for soul care. The thunder of crashing waves gently kissed the seashore. The rhythmic brilliance from the beacon of light summoned those adrift into safe harbor. The Lord brought me to a holy place.

I took my coffee out to the water's edge and checked my online devotion for my daily inspiration. A notification led me to a friend's birthday message. She wrote about discovering her birth Scripture—Romans 8:28.

I'd never heard of a personal birth Scripture before. I wondered which verse my April seventeenth birthday would lead me to. After bypassing a couple 4:17 passages, I landed on 2 Timothy 4:17 (NIV): "But the Lord stood at my side and gave me strength, so that through me the message might be fully proclaimed and all the Gentiles might hear it. And I was delivered from the lion's mouth."

My curiosity and desire for understanding led me to read the surrounding passages to gain proper context. Paul explained how only God came to his defense and spared his life. Why? The Lord called Paul to proclaim the gospel and nothing or nobody could prevent that from happening. The next verse promised that God would rescue him from every evil attack and guide him safely to heaven.

I paused, mesmerized. The sunrise brightened the new day with glorious hues of gold over the ocean. The Lord whispered to my heart. *You were never an outcast. You were set apart as my beloved. I'm not only here with you to give you the strength you need to do this, but I've always been with you from before the day you were born. Yes, it was I who held your hand, never letting go, every step of the way. I did all those things you wonder about.*

In that profound moment, the Lord unveiled the true extent of the endurance and triumphs of the little girl in me, like a symphony of emotions playing in my heart. My life, seen through a heavenly lens, transcended mere survival into a spiritual transformative journey, like old photographs rejuvenated with vibrant colors. Soft whispers from the Holy Spirit continued to touch my soul. *I led you to the wilderness. It was there you had to rediscover my love for you, like you knew* years before. Only in that place of aloneness could you fully realize you are my beloved.

A sense of assurance and discovery left me breathless. Exactly where I lost myself is where Jesus found me. On the deck of the lighthouse, I stood above the ocean's edge. Mesmerized by the waters crashing into the rugged shoreline, I gripped the weathered wood railing.

Breathing in the vastness of His love, I closed my eyes. Thank you, Lord … for choosing me as Your beloved, for embracing me with Your divine grace and unwavering affection, for remaining my husband all those years, for cherishing me. Thank you for guiding me through the use of my gifts into a life of purpose. In Your love, I find strength, solace, and belonging. May your light continue to guide my steps. Jesus, I am eternally your Beloved, and my Beloved is mine. Amen.

Afterword

In this world of groups, tribes, clubs, affiliations, parties, and denominations, we tend to sacrifice who we are so we may satisfy our primal yearning for belonging. According to Brené Brown, a social scientist, our sense of belonging can never be greater than our level of self-acceptance.

This presents a conundrum. If we continue to sacrifice ourselves, we will never know true belonging as God's Beloved. The same thing applies when we mask our true identity with self-rejection or internal lies. My own lack of self-worth led me to doubt all the good things the Bible said about me. This skewed my perception of myself. Viewing ourselves through a lens of brokenness sets us on a path of displaced loyalties and further rejection.

I understand the soul's need for belonging. Those entrusted with my safety only brought calamity. Amid it all, I found myself grappling with doubts about my true self, the authenticity of my relationships, the definition of love, and where I truly belonged. This manifested through self-destructive behavior, self-loathing, complex post-traumatic stress disorder (C-PTSD), cutting, hopelessness, and constant striving to find a safe place to belong. I wore many masks, each one carefully crafted to ensure my survival.

What appeared impossible to overcome led me on a journey of discovery. I faced my demons head-on. I learned God desires the outcast and rejected soul to experience life as His Beloved. Through baptism in the Holy Spirit, we can establish an authentic connection with Jesus, discovering our belovedness and finding true peace and belonging. Paul wrote in 1 Corinthians 12:3 "No one can say, "Jesus is Lord" except by the Holy Spirit." God's truth cuts through the bars of iron and frees us. We are pulled from our blindness so we may see ourselves as His Beloved.

I learned that revisiting a painful story serves one or two purposes: The writing journey is intended as a means of catharsis or the story acts as a key to unlock someone else's prison. My hope is my story serves both.

The writing of *Beloved Outcast* was a gift. A gift to God, His gift to me, and a gift for you. Five years of drafts, edits, pauses, and rewrites kept me revisiting past trauma over and over again. From the beginning of this undertaking, I reminded myself of the task to which I must remain obedient. Not out of obligation, but from an unwavering devotion to God. I did not anticipate the breaking open of my soul only to have my foundation strengthened through glorious moments of emotional and spiritual restoration.

I am writing the last few words in this Afterword on Christmas Eve 2023. I gift this story to Jesus and commit to Holy Spirit the outcome of this project. Despite the difficulty of sharing my darkest, most painful memories, I am privileged to bear witness to the profound encounters of rescue, rebirth, renewal, and complete rebranding of my soul. God's justice redeems the unfathomable. He authored this story more than me.

Hope, healing, forgiveness, and deliverance can be found in these pages. I hope my story serves as a life-altering message and guiding light on your transformative journey into a life as His Beloved.

Acknowledgments

For naming me 'Beloved' and calling me His own, for the gift of grit-fueled faith, for His continual pursuit and rescue, and for His Spirit who works overtime on my heart, I am forever grateful to my Lord and Savior, Jesus Christ. I felt a divine calling to write this book. I couldn't have done so without Him.

I am grateful my mother, Rosemary Lynn Street, nurtured my love for reading and writing. She kept me from giving up on my dreams. My mom helped me write the early chapters. Though we painfully stumbled through them, my mother remains my greatest cheerleader.

My father, Arther Peter LaLanne, who rests in 'the place that's the best,' took great joy in telling me stories for my book. I look forward to seeing him again in heaven. To my loving stepmother, Rose Mills, I am forever grateful for her unconditional love and prayers.

I extend my heartfelt gratitude to my lifelong friends whose ongoing source of blessings helped unearth happy memories. Arlene Soske, Diana Soske (McCredy), Dorothy Soske (Rael), John Simpson, Heidi Wedeking (Williams), you all hold a special place in my heart as my dearest childhood friends and family.

Like many, I am beyond blessed to have at least one person in my life who prayerfully reaches for me and loves me through the darkness without running scared. Monica Dalton-Melendez loved me too much to *not* introduce me to Jesus. I pray she is richly rewarded for the blessings she has poured into my life through her love and prayers.

Sisters sometimes come into our life in unexpected ways. Though we started out as friends, Cindy Scanlan and I became sisters while we walked alongside one another through parallel seasons of loss. Only God can birth a bond which imparts a knowing and understanding of another's soul. Cindy championed me throughout this project.

With the deepest love and heartfelt gratitude, I honor Lorraine Dennis, Barbara Donaldson, and Donal Meeks, ministry leaders at Cathedral of Faith in San Jose, California. They facilitated the annual women's retreat held at Mission Springs Christian Camp and Conference Center in Scotts Valley, California, which I attended for five consecutive years.

For my Lakeside Church family in Folsom, California, I owe a debt of gratitude. Pastor Jim Price saw something in this misfit outlaw and discipled me into ministry leadership. For all the prayer warriors who bombarded the gates of heaven on my behalf, I am grateful. I'll remain eternally grateful for the leader of our prayer team, Bob Nelson. His grit-fueled faith was contagious and is the faith I will always desire.

Some of my most memorable times of spiritual growth came from witnessing the faith of Maribeth Sexton. Likewise, my dear angel of a friend, Joan Gross, whose lifetime of heartwarming Jesus testimonies sowed seeds of hope into my heart. Their treasured belovedness bestowed upon me a goal to attain.

To the friends who opened their home, providing a haven for my daughter and me during our brief season of homelessness: Maribeth Sexton, Diane and Dan Osier, Cindy and Ron Dickson, and Lisa

Ferrante-Swanson. I am forever grateful for their genuine fellowship and love.

Huge thanks to Pastor Nancy Atchley and my friends at Powerhouse Ministries in Folsom, California, for their love, discipleship, and prayers that provided the tools and resources to heal, and a place to belong while serving fellow outcasts.

I am sincerely grateful for my brother, pastor, and ministry partner, Johnny Lujan, for his passion for the outcast and the incredible opportunity to plant Thunder Road Biker Church of Northern California. Partnering with Teen Challenge is an experience I'll always hold close to my heart.

Mission Springs Christian Camp and Conference Center in Scotts Valley, California, served as the primary location for writing most of this manuscript. My utmost appreciation and gratitude go to Pastor Chuck Wysong and the staff for their prayers, accommodations, and support.

I'm grateful to my Life Community Church family for their prayers, counsel, and encouragement throughout the process of writing my story.

And to the precious sisters from my Bible study group from Life Community Church, led by Sue Olsen, I am grateful for all their prayers, support, and encouragement. We studied Shadia Hrichi's Bible study, *Hagar: Rediscovering the God Who Sees Me*, while I worked on the draft of my manuscript. The Holy Spirit sustained and strengthened my hand through each chapter. Shadia became a dear friend, and I am beyond grateful for her influence and prayers.

Attending my first Christian writers conference, the Mount Hermon Christian Writers Conference in Scotts Valley, California, changed everything for me in my journey toward publication. My heartfelt gratitude to Janet Thompson for her memoir mentoring clinic where she imparted gems of wisdom of the writing craft. She became one of the strongest advocates of my story.

It's difficult to express the depth of gratitude for my dear friend and soul sister, Phylis Mantelli, whom I met in Janet Thompson's memoir mentoring clinic. After losing my digital files, Phylis's encouragement gave me the strength to start over. She championed my story and has supported me through her encouragement, prayers, and brutal honesty.

From the very start of this book project, my dear friend Dori DeVries Harrell provided invaluable coaching in refining the raw version of my manuscript. She poured her prayerful heart and soul into my story. I am forever grateful for our friendship.

For their generous and loving hearts and for sharing invaluable knowledge of the writing craft, my heartfelt thanks to Edie Melson, DiAnn Mills, Linda Goldfarb, Edwina Perkins, Eva Marie Everson, and the rest of the team at the Blue Ridge Mountains Christian Writers Conference.

I have utmost appreciation for my sisters from the Advanced Writers and Speakers Association (AWSA) and for my mentor through their Protégé Program, Amber Weigand-Buckley. She is a kindred spirit, friend, and the most generous encourager who uses her platform to raise the voice of others.

Sometimes God sends a dove to safely guide us in our calling. Tremendous gratitude goes to Karen and George Porter, Amber Weigand-Buckley, Rhonda Rhea, Larry J. Leech II (my editor), and the rest of the publishing board at Bold Vision Books for believing in and championing my story. Larry's mastery of the writing craft, combined with his gifting to discern the emotional and spiritual impact of my message, leaves me in awe. It is an honor and a privilege to publish my first book with Bold Vision Books.

Angelica, my daughter, is a gift from God. We share a passion for writing, and her encouragement and support throughout this project mean more to me than she will ever know.

And to my husband and purpose mate, Mike, there are no words to describe how grateful I am for his prompting, "What do you need to finish the book God has asked you to write?" He never once questioned the timing or the investment which also included frequent writing getaways to "the pond" (a.k.a. the ocean). Mike's servant heart and sacrificial love were a constant lifeline while battling emotional triggers and doubting my ability to finish this story. He even called in the prayer troops when I did not have the strength to return to the page. I love him deeply for partnering with me, celebrating the victories, and devoting our marriage to Kingdom work.

Resources And Helps

A.C.E. Score at Your Number Story–https://numberstory.org/

Trauma Research Foundation–https://traumaresearchfoundation.org/

Relapse Prevention–The Genesis Process–https://www.genesisprocess.org/

The Body Keeps the Score–https://www.besselvanderkolk.com/resources/the-body-keeps-the-score

Trauma Research & Helps–https://www.besselvanderkolk.com/resources/in-the-media

Alcoholics Anonymous–https://www.aa.org/

Narcotics Anonymous–https://na.org/

Celebrate Recovery–https://www.celebraterecovery.com/

Adult & Teen Challenge–https://teenchallengeusa.org/

Darkness to Light – Childhood Sexual Abuse Advocacy/Training–https://www.d2l.org/

Darkness to Light–Stewards of Children–https://www.thenewstewards.org/

Freedom Through Education–https://www.freedomthrougheducation.com/

AbuseCare–https://www.abusecare.org/about/

Bloom In the Dark–https://bloominthedark.org/

About the Author

CHERIE DENNA is an author, speaker, and writing coach who has served for more than twelve years in women's ministry, relapse prevention, and various leadership positions.

An award-winning writer, Cherie Denna's messages empower audiences to adorn the shadowy, often stigmatized pages of their story with the power of truth. In a world of isolation and injustice, Cherie's desire is to help others persevere, be known, belong, and be loved. She loves Jesus, her purpose-mate husband, and frothed coffee at the ocean.

Cherie's works include several collaborations and online devotionals including Arise Daily (AWSA).

She also writes a relevant blog at https://cheriedenna.com.